TOURISM
BUSINESS DIAGNOSTICS

FRANK BOURREE
RICHARD MIMICK
MICHAEL THOMSON

Note for Librarians: A cataloguing record for this book is available from Library and Archives Canada at www.collectionscanada.ca/amicus/index-e.html

ISBN 1-4120-7509-2

Design, typesetting and cover: R. Diment VRG
www.members.shaw.ca/vrg
Cover image courtesy: Long Beach Lodge Resort

Printed in Victoria, BC, Canada. Printed on paper with minimum 30% recycled fibre. Trafford's print shop runs on "green energy" from solar, wind and other environmentally-friendly power sources.

TRAFFORD
PUBLISHING™

Offices in Canada, USA, Ireland and UK

This book was published *on-demand* in cooperation with Trafford Publishing. On-demand publishing is a unique process and service of making a book available for retail sale to the public taking advantage of on-demand manufacturing and Internet marketing. On-demand publishing includes promotions, retail sales, manufacturing, order fulfilment, accounting and collecting royalties on behalf of the author.

Book sales for North America and international:
Trafford Publishing, 6E–2333 Government St.,
Victoria, BC v8t 4p4 CANADA
phone 250 383 6864 (toll-free 1 888 232 4444)
fax 250 383 6804; email to orders@trafford.com

Book sales in Europe:
Trafford Publishing (uk) Limited, 9 Park End Street, 2nd Floor
Oxford, UK ox1 1hh UNITED KINGDOM
phone 44 (0)1865 722 113 (local rate 0845 230 9601)
facsimile 44 (0)1865 722 868; info.uk@trafford.com

Order online at:
trafford.com/05-2405

10 9 8 7 6 5 4 3 2

ABOUT
THE AUTHORS

Frank Bourree, CMC, is a Partner and the leader of Grant Thornton LLP Tourism Consulting Services based in Victoria, BC.

He has more than 30 years of experience in the tourism industry and has provided operational, start-up guidance, repositioning strategies, business and strategic planning to governments, resorts, hotels, restaurants and golf course operations.

His specialties include tourism studies; business valuations; tourism executive search; franchise consultation; and multi-unit operations. Frank has completed over 100 business valuations and feasibility studies and has participated in numerous lease and purchase-and-sale negotiations and resort developments.

Before joining the firm, Frank was the BC Regional Manager for Controlled Foods International (Earls, Corkscrews, Fullers and A&W). In 1983 he purchased the franchise rights to six Vancouver Island A&W franchisees, which he expanded to 10 units and then sold in 1993. During his tenure with A&W, he pioneered and chaired its BC Regional Advertising Association, served on its National Advertising Council and Building Design Advisory Team, and was decorated Victoria's Restaurateur of the Year in 1986.

Previously, Frank was Director of the Tourism Consulting for the Victoria office of Price Waterhouse prior to the merger with Grant Thornton. He has served on the Boards of Tourism BC, Tourism Victoria, Global TV Advisory Board, Victoria Chamber of Commerce and is active with the Tourism Industry Association and Hotel Associations of Canada.

Rich Mimick is President and CEO of PPM Professional Practice Management Inc, a management consulting and executive development firm based in Victoria, BC. Rich was formerly a CPA (USA) and commenced his consulting career with Andersen Consulting.

His academic appointments include Chair and Professor at the world ranked Ivey Business School, Director of Royal Roads University Business Programs, Director of University of Victoria's Executive Programs and Director, Business Management and Technology, Division of Continuing Studies, University of Victoria.

Rich has designed, developed and delivered consulting engagements and executive programs for Canadian, American, European and Asian clients. His areas of expertise are strategic management, finance and marketing strategy.

He has received international recognition for his outstanding teaching and is known for his exceptional ability to turn complex topics into understandable practical learning.

Rich also provides consulting assistance in strategy and finance to various companies. He is a director and advisory board member of growth oriented companies and a past director of VIATeC, the Vancouver Island Advanced Technology Centre.

Mike Thompson, CMC, has over 20 years of commercial banking experience gained in the UK, Ontario and British Columbia, Canada.

He is presently Professor of Management Consulting at Royal Roads University in Victoria. Prior to assuming this position, he was Senior Manager, Business Development for a Canadian commercial bank, located in Victoria, British Columbia.

His academic credentials include an Honors degree in Economics from the University of Manchester and a Diploma in Land Economics from the University of British Columbia.

Professional certifications include Fellow of Institute of Canadian Bankers (FICB) and Certified Management Consultant.

Mike has taught Business Strategy courses at both the University of Victoria and Royal Roads University and has developed a number of successful business planning and risk assessment seminars for business and professional associations.

He is actively involved in the Victoria business community and is presently a Director of the Innovation and Development Corporation (IDC) at the University of Victoria.

CONTENTS

SECTION 1   THE EXTERNAL 'SIZE-UP'
Chapter 1 The Business Environment 3
Chapter 2 Industry Conditions 19

SECTION 2   THE INTERNAL 'SIZE-UP'
Chapter 3 The Financial Evaluation 33
Chapter 4 Marketing Strategy 65
Chapter 5 The Operations Review 79
Chapter 6 Human Resources Management 101
Chapter 7 The Technology Assessment 115

SECTION 3   THE COMPANY LIFE CYCLE AND RELATED FUNDING INITIATIVES
Chapter 8 New Business Opportunities and Strategies 131
Chapter 9 Sources of Equity Funding 147
Chapter 10 Managing Growth 159
Chapter 11 Sources of Debt Financing 165
Chapter 12 Survival Strategies 185

SECTION 4   STRATEGIC PLANNING
Chapter 13 Business and Strategic Plans 195

SECTION 5   CASE STUDY
The Inn on Cortes Island 211

APPENDIX 1   EXTERNAL AND INTERNAL 'SIZE-UP'
             THE INN ON CORTES ISLAND 235

APPENDIX 2   ENTERPRISE REVIEW SUMMARY (ERS)
             FOR THE INN ON CORTES ISLAND LTD 247

APPENDIX 3   COMMERCIAL BANKING RISK ASSESSMENT
             FOR THE INN ON CORTES ISLAND LTD 255

REFERENCES AND RECOMMENDED READINGS 259

PREFACE AND ACKNOWLEDGMENTS

The genesis of the original **Business Diagnostics** concept can be traced to an early evening libation at Spinnakers Brew Pub, Victoria, BC in April 1995. Rich and Mike were both teaching a 'fast track' business strategy course for the University of Victoria and had been discussing the need to quickly and simply summarize business concepts for not only adult learners, but also business owners as well.

We decided to design a short, but informative business case and then perform a 'size up' on the subject company, assessing the relative attractiveness of the external environment and internal resources. This discussion led to the development of a successful one-day seminar series, which was anchored by a companion manual –"Size-Up Your Business".

The research and writing of the original **Business Diagnostics** book took place between April 2000 and February 2001.We received tremendous support and encouragement from the Victoria business community and have since successfully introduced the text to business programs at the University of Victoria and Royal Roads University. The book has also been well received by local business owners and members of the CGA and CA accounting professions.

Frank Bourree, a senior Partner with Grant Thornton LLP, had been a strong and encouraging supporter of the **Business Diagnostics** model and after some discussions in late 2004, it was agreed that a Tourism edition would be an exciting and worthwhile initiative.

The following people have provided wonderful support in the completion of this new edition:

Deborah Wickins did a superb job in updating the book to include current and relevant tourism sector materials along with the provision of valuable HR insights into the new case study.

Tim Hackett, owner of Long Beach Lodge, Tolfino, provided some pragmatic insights and graciously allowed us to use a photograph of his resort property on our cover.

Grant Thornton staff in the Victoria office made a significant contribution to the tourism content, in particular: Charles Shier, CA; Christine Stoneman, CMC; Dinah White, M.A.; Carolyn Yeager and Lasha Elkuf.

The case study review process was greatly simplified by helpful feedback from Deb Linehan, Area Manager, Royal Bank, Victoria, B.C and Alex McKenzie, former National Director, Commercial Mortgages, Bank of Montreal, Toronto, Ontario. Additional helpful input was provided by Jake Posliff, TD Canada Trust, and Peter Christensen, TD Commercial Banking

Roy Diment (*Vivencia Resources Group*) completed the book graphic design and layout while Bruce Batchelor, CEO, *Trafford Publishing*, provided wise counsel and support through the publishing process.

Last but certainly not least, special thanks and acknowledgment is given to our respective spouses, Janice, Claudia and Kathy, for their patience and cheerful encouragement.

Frank Bourree, Richard Mimick, and Michael Thompson

Victoria, BC
March 2006

INTRODUCTION

The original **Business Diagnostics** text was written to overcome a significant challenge facing today's business owners: specifically, the time constraints in acquiring business management skills. Business owners have limited time or inclination to attend extended business school courses. Likewise, accessing topical information on enhancing corporate performance (magazines or websites) can be sporadic and time consuming. The authors designed **Business Diagnostics** to address these concerns by developing a valuable reference book that can be easily read over a weekend or a few weekday evenings.

Since its original publication in 2001, **Business Diagnostics** has proven to be an effective reference and business tool in a variety of settings. Building on this success, and acknowledging the importance of the tourism industry in Canada, the authors decided to create a version of the book that more specifically addressed the issues and dynamics facing tourism and hospitality managers today.

The material presented here will provide a fast track to understanding the fundamentals and challenges in running and growing a tourism company. Readers will gain practical insights into the following key areas:

Sections 1 and 2: Instruct the reader how to 'size up' a tourism business operation, assessing its relative strengths and weaknesses.

> The External size-up examines the business environment (political, economic, societal and technological factors) along with prevailing industry conditions.

> The Internal size-up then drills down into the individual company's performance, evaluating its relative health from different viewpoints – Financial, Marketing, Operations, Human Resources, and Technology.

Section 3: Explains company life cycles and how various sources of funding (equity and debt) can be accessed. Survival and turnaround strategies are also evaluated. Recognizing potential danger signals is increasingly important given today's rapidly changing business environment.

Section 4: Provides tips and insights on the effective completion of Business and Strategy plans.

Section 5: Consists of a short case study of a fictitious company – the Inn on Cortes Island. Readers utilize the size up techniques covered in earlier sections to assess the company's health and prospects by completing optional size-up work sheets as part of the evaluation process.

Tourism Business Diagnostics will provide practical assistance to the following target audiences:

> ➤ The individual who wishes to set up a new, yet to be proven, tourism venture and requires guidelines to assess the likelihood of success and the steps necessary to attract financing or equity.

> ➤ The existing tourism business owner or manager who has growth opportunities and needs to 'size up' existing and potential operations.

> ➤ The individual planning to buy or invest in another business. That process requires the completion of 'diagnostic checks' to ensure that the targeted entity has the required degree of corporate health.

> ➤ A new or existing tourism company owner who needs to assess the relative merits of attracting outside equity capital or raising additional debt in order to expand product lines and/or markets in the tourism sector.

Tourism operators may find that some **Tourism Business Diagnostics** content may not relate specifically to their own operations. In particular, the chapters dedicated to the discussion of technology and raising equity may be of limited relevance to smaller operators in the tourism sector. However, this original content has been retained in this new edition, as a tool and reference for larger hospitality businesses, and to give valuable broad context to the overall business environment today.

SECTION 1

THE EXTERNAL 'SIZE-UP'

CHAPTER 1
THE BUSINESS ENVIRONMENT

OVERVIEW

A key element of the External Size-Up process is looking at 'The Big Picture'. The prevailing business environment and related industry conditions need to be critically reviewed by company management.

This chapter covers the Business Environment. Think of it as an outer atmosphere that, while distinct from day-to-day company operations, exerts a significant impact on a company's prospects and performance.

A useful tool to assess the Business Environment is a P.E.S.T. analysis, an easy-to-remember acronym that encompasses the following four key areas:

- Political Factors

- Economic Issues

- Societal Factors

- Technological Considerations

Each key area is reviewed, providing a checklist of issues to consider. While some of these issues are industry specific (i.e., they relate to the industry within which a company operates or is associated), the focus of this chapter remains the big picture.

The P.E.S.T. structure and the impact on an individual company are illustrated in Figure 1-1 below:

Figure 1-1

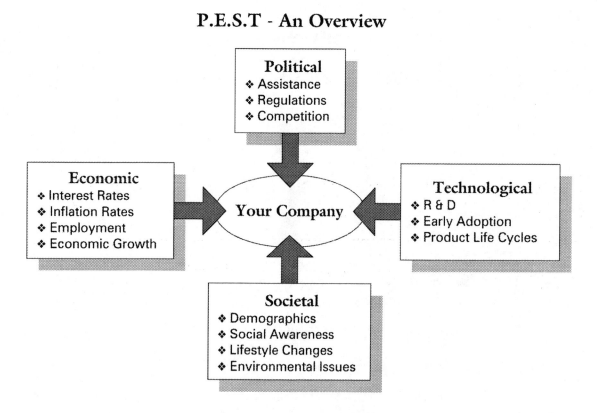

P.E.S.T - An Overview

Political
- ❖ Assistance
- ❖ Regulations
- ❖ Competition

Economic
- ❖ Interest Rates
- ❖ Inflation Rates
- ❖ Employment
- ❖ Economic Growth

Your Company

Technological
- ❖ R & D
- ❖ Early Adoption
- ❖ Product Life Cycles

Societal
- ❖ Demographics
- ❖ Social Awareness
- ❖ Lifestyle Changes
- ❖ Environmental Issues

POLITICAL FACTORS

The predominant force in political factors affecting a business is government influence, ranging from federal to provincial to municipal, or a combination of all three. You should be aware that governments can:

- ➤ Assist you

- ➤ Regulate you

- ➤ Compete with you

Consider your company and the environment in which it operates, and then review the following checklist to determine the extent to which government activities influence your business environment. It is also worthwhile to assess the extent of business-friendly policies implemented by your federal, provincial and municipal governments.

> Is new legislation pending that may change their approach to regulating business?

> Will the political climate change in the near term? What impact will this have on your business?

The hospitality industry is affected by government at all three levels. At the federal level, there are six government departments that directly affect the tourism industry.

> Industry Canada is responsible for the overall well-being of the tourism industry. Working as a Crown corporation under the auspices of this department is the Canadian Tourism Commission which became a Crown Corporation in 2001.

> The Department of Foreign Affairs and International Trade is responsible for issuing Canadian passports and visas for non-Canadians.

> Canada Customs and Revenue Agency handles Canada Customs.

> Citizenship and Immigration Canada verifies the travel documents of returning Canadian travelers and foreign visitors. Both Immigration and Customs officials play an important role in creating a positive first impression for tourists.

> Canadian Heritage is responsible for Parks Canada, National Historic Sites and Battlefields, National Museums and Archives, and the National Capital Commission.

> Transport Canada oversees the regulation of our transportation systems and helps with the building and maintenance of the transportation infrastructure.[1]

Provincially, there are ministries or departments whose mandates are to promote travel and increase visitor traffic to each province, to develop the tourism industry overall through market research, and liaise with industry and other levels of government. Finally, on a municipal level, some cities also offer tourism marketing departments or convention/visitor bureaus. In areas that are highly dependent upon tourism for their local economies, Destination Marketing Organizations (DMO's) and local Chambers of Commerce may also be involved in the promotion of local businesses to attract visitors.

GOVERNMENT ASSISTANCE TO BUSINESS

Government support – through special programs, funding, education, and more – may make a difference to your business operations. It is a worthwhile investment of time to determine whether government support is available for:

> Financing

> Employment programs

> Technological innovation

> Industrial research, or

> Export opportunities.

Remember

If grants and/or subsidies are available, they may also be available to your competitors. You must also determine whether there any strings attached.

For tourism operators, there are a variety of federal government programs that can assist with financial or employment assistance.[2] Further, the creation of the Canadian Tourism Commission (CTC) has also had a significant impact upon the industry's relationship with government. Forging a partnership with both provincial governments and industry, the resulting CTC has allowed for important opportunities to coordinate programs that benefit Canada's tourism industry overall. Industry matches government promotional spending, dollar for dollar.

Although the CTC does not lobby government, or provide actual grants or subsidies, the partnership has benefited Canadian hospitality businesses by creating national databases and statistics, launching a series of marketing campaigns on an international scale, and providing research and analysis on both domestic and international market opportunities and issues.

At the provincial/territorial level, there are often programs and publications that a hospitality operator can access that can be helpful to their operations. Some provinces also offer employment programs that are specific to the tourism industry, such as the Destinations Tourism Employment Program in BC (www.destinations.ca). Please see the end of the chapter for a list of Canadian provincial tourism websites and other government resources.

REGULATION OF BUSINESS

How do the following regulatory mechanisms impact your business?

> ➤ Taxation: can reduce your return on investment and may increase or decrease your competitive advantage if your company faces lower or higher tax rates than your competition.

> ➤ Health and safety legislation and regulations. This is particularly important within the food and beverage sector, both for customers and employees. New laws concerning alcohol consumption and smoking restrictions have had significant impact on tourism operators in recent years, affecting insurance premiums and even the way they do business.

> ➤ Environmental policies and controls: incentives, fees, penalties, potential project delays.

> ➤ Regulating competition: an example is the Federal Competition Act which prohibits certain practices like tied selling, exclusive dealing, discriminatory allowances, etc.

> ➤ Consumer protection: examples would include the Food and Drug Act and the Hazardous Products Act.

> ➤ Investor protection: various securities acts.

> ➤ Protecting employee rights. In the tourism sector, employers are faced with unique circumstances that define the labour market. Many tourism jobs are entry-level positions, often held by young people and students. Nonetheless, such employees are critical to the success of an organization because of their high level of face to face interaction with clients. New initiatives within the industry have focused on employee satisfaction and retention, through regulation and training programs. Also, demographics are having an impact whereupon older retirees and second household income earners are also being attracted to the industry.

> ➤ Protection of firms' intangible assets: trademarks, patents, copyrights, and industrial design.

DIRECT COMPETITION WITH BUSINESS

At times, government can be a source of competition for your business.

> ➤ Crown Corporations (government-owned) can be unpredictable competitors with deep pockets. Examples are Via Rail and Parks Canada.

> ➤ Privatization of government agencies can intensify competitive pressures by altering traditional buying and selling practices. For example, some British Columbia tourism operators fear that the privatization of BC Ferries might push fares beyond the price point that some travelers are willing to pay, thus lowering traffic levels on many routes, particularly in the Gulf Islands, that are dependent upon ferry traffic for their livelihood.

ECONOMIC ISSUES

The state of the economy has an obvious impact on your business. For tourism operators, the economic havoc wreaked worldwide in the aftermath of September 11, 2001 has demonstrated this cause-and-effect all too clearly. The war in Iraq and SARS outbreaks have also had tremendous impacts on world economies. Yet, many business owners are confused by the overwhelming weight of economic data and information available to them.

There are hundreds of economic indicators published on a regular basis by financial and economic analysts and government agencies. The challenge is to identify the relevant ones for your business, and to use them effectively. This section separates the trees from the forest by summarizing the six key areas of macro economic activity that will impact the business owner.

KEY MACROECONOMIC INDICATORS

1. Economic Growth

2. Price levels (inflation)

3. International exchange rates

4. Interest rates

5. Employment

6. Government policy

7. Global economic influences

1. ECONOMIC GROWTH

➤ The primary indicator of economic growth is Gross Domestic Product (GDP), which measures a country's economic output. Real GDP recognizes that the effect of inflation on price levels has been removed, thereby providing a more accurate fix on actual economic growth.

➤ Until recently, GDP growth rates of 3-4% in North America indicated robust, growing economies accompanied by strong consumer confidence and spending.

➤ Three consecutive (three-month) quarters of decline in GDP growth are generally considered to indicate the onset of a recession. Tourism is an industry that is heavily reliant upon a healthy economic climate. In times of recession, the tourism sector has sharply felt the downturns, as potential travelers have had to turn their attention back to basics, rather than on "extras" such as leisure travel.

➤ Three macro motivations for travel are business (corporate, commercial, convention, meeting, government, educational); pleasure (tourist, leisure, escape); and personal (death, health, religious). Economic factors impact these groups differently.

2. PRICE LEVELS

➤ The prevailing level of price inflation has a crucial effect on consumer confidence, business revenue and earnings performance.

➤ The primary inflation indicator is the Consumer Price Index (CPI). The CPI measures the relative price increases of a 'basket' of goods and services. (The index's accuracy has been questioned in the past for its susceptibility to interest rate swings, short-term erratic price fluctuations, and the extent to which energy and food costs have been included.)

➤ Inflation can be broadly segmented as follows:

i) Demand Pull: Prices are 'pulled' up by strong consumer and business demand for goods and services. Demand for tourism products tends to be quite elastic; price sensitivity is high, since leisure travel is still considered a luxury product by many people. Demand for high-end tourism products tends to be quite elastic; price sensitivity is high, since certain leisure travel niches are still considered a luxury product by many people. "The tourism industry learned this lesson with the new millennium celebrations. Overpriced products remained unsold, hotel rooms were left vacant, and huge parties were cancelled due to poor sales."[3]

One needs to remember that different leisure experiences, on a spectrum of luxury to basic, will have differing price points and elasticities.

ii) Cost Push: Prices are 'pushed' up by increased raw material and labour costs. For example, an increase in the provincial minimum wage can have a significant impact on pricing schemes used by hospitality businesses.

3. INTERNATIONAL EXCHANGE RATES

> The tourism industry globally is particularly sensitive to fluctuations in international exchange rates. In Canada, many destinations are heavily reliant upon high volumes of American and international visitors. When the Canadian dollar is strong, there is a double impact: more Canadians choose to travel internationally, and fewer international visitors choose to come here when Canada is no longer the "bargain" it once may have been. There are trickle-down effects as well: different spending habits between Canadians and Americans make the food service industry particularly vulnerable to fewer visits by U.S. tourists in Canada. A 2004 study revealed the following contrasts:

	United States	Canada
Per capita disposable income:	$34,302	$22,827
Restaurant share of household food dollar:	42%	30.3%
Average check size per person:	$7.26	$5.98[4]

4. INTEREST RATES

> Interest rates are a key influence on economic activity. Both short-term and long-term rates need to be considered.

> Short-term rates (one to twelve months) are set by the Bank of Canada and/or the U.S. Federal Reserve Bank and exert a significant impact on consumer credit and business borrowings.

> Long-term rates (one to twenty years) follow corporate and government bond markets. These rates have a major impact on consumer big-ticket purchases and business expansion/capital expenditure decisions.

> The relationship between short-term and long-term interest rates has historically been defined by a positive yield curve with short-term rates lower than long-term rates (investors require a greater reward to lock in investments for a longer time period).

➤ An inverted yield curve (short-term rates higher than long-term rates) is often considered to be a precursor to a recession.

Figure 1-2 below provides a graphical representation of positive and negative yield curves.

Figure 1-2 Yield Curves

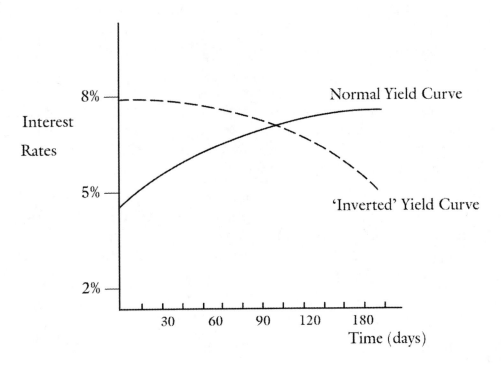

➤ Interest rates may have a significant impact on a company's financial performance and strategies. For example, in a rising interest rate environment, the company's ability to repay debt will be impaired (higher interest costs, less principal paid back).

➤ Even if an early stage company has been funded by equity (as opposed to debt financing), increasing interest rates will tend to exert a dampening effect on overall economic growth prospects.

4. EMPLOYMENT

➤ The primary indicator of labour market health is the percentage of the available workforce that is unemployed. Rates close to the 3-4% level indicate 'full employment'.

> There are significant differences in the kinds of employment experienced by workers and the resulting impact on the economy. Some are:

> i) Frictional unemployment: Workers temporarily out of work, often due to seasonal factors (eg., ski hill operators at Whistler).

> ii) Cyclical unemployment: Workers without jobs due to downturns in business cycles (e.g., tourism, real estate sales, shipbuilding, auto sector).

> iii) Structural unemployment: People out of work for long periods of time due to lack of skills (e.g., pursuing higher education) or fundamental changes in economic resources (e.g., forestry, east coast fisheries).

Tourism employment faces a number of critical issues. Changing demographics have resulted in a labour shortage for traditional tourism jobs, retention is more difficult, due in part to the cyclical nature of many business, and skills shortages present further challenges. These issues are explored in more detail in Chapter 6.

A high unemployment rate in a community or area is positive for tourism from the perspective of accessing staff, but not for tourism services receiving local spending. Conversely, a low unemployment rate means difficulty for tourism businesses to attract potential employees because they are competing with other industries for staff.

5. GOVERNMENT ACTIVITIES AND POLICIES

Consider:

> The current levels of direct and indirect taxes compared to competitors' countries. Taxation has been a contentious issue for the hospitality industry in Canada. For every dollar spent on tourism in Canada, in 2002 there was a "yield [of] about 17 cents to the Government of Canada and 31 cents to all order of government combined."[5] There have been benefits for some operators, such as hotels that charge a room tax, and then use the funds generated to better market their location.

> On a broader scale, however, the high level of taxation in our country, particularly after the GST was introduced in 1991, can make Canada a less appealing destination compared to other countries whose taxation schemes are less onerous. Nonetheless, some gains have been won by the Tourism Industry Association of Canada: visitors to Canada can now claim back their GST paid, and international conferences no longer pay the GST when they choose Canada as their destination.

> ➤ The potential for transfer payment cutbacks (federal to provincial to municipal governments).

> ➤ The level of government spending which is affected by current fiscal budget performance.

Following September 11, 2001, regulations pertaining to the transportation industry underwent major changes/enhancements. With the laudable goal of making travel more secure, some tourists and import/export operators have nonetheless found the additional bureaucracy (additional security checks, use of new scanning equipment/techniques, additional checkpoints and paperwork at borders of crossing) to be time consuming and inconvenient.

Other concerns have arisen regarding the cost of security. In Canada, a new Air Travellers Security Charge of $12.50 per passenger was levied to pay for enhanced security initiatives. However, according to the Airline Industry Monitoring Consortium in BC, this has "cost B.C. voters $73.5 million in tourism spending and 1,340 jobs each year".[6]

6. GLOBAL ECONOMIC INFLUENCES

Key areas to assess:

> ➤ Currency value: In the tourism sector, the availability of a common worldwide "currency" – the credit card – and the advent of Automated Teller Machines throughout the world have eliminated much of the hassle of currency exchange during international travel.

> From a business perspective, where the target market is foreign versus domestic, the relative value of the Canadian versus the U.S. dollar and other currencies such as the Euro has a major impact on exporters and importers, and the relative attractiveness of travelling domestically versus internationally.

> While short-term fluctuations are difficult to anticipate, longer-term trends can often be identified and hedged against by forward exchange rate contracts available through your bank.

> ➤ Trading arrangements: Be aware of free trade areas versus economies that remain protected by tariffs and quotas. Examples include the North American Free Trade Agreement (NAFTA) and the European Community (EC). Of particular interest to the tourism sector is the Open Skies arrangement that Canada has had with the U.S. since 1995, which allows airlines in both countries to establish direct routings between any two cities located on either

side of the border. The 2010 Olympics is also an example of an international agreement that impacts the tourism infrastructure.

- ➤ Global markets: The rise of monopolistic multinationals with enormous buying power and economies of scale. For example, international consolidation within the hotel industry has demonstrated the power of brand names within a global context. Expanding to even the budget hotel market, companies such as Comfort Inn and Best Western have acquired properties around the world in an effort to access the market of North American tourists in international locales, and also to achieve higher economies of scale from expanding their operations.

- ➤ Preferential treatment: Countries imposing 'buy at home' policies on government departments and agencies to ensure local companies have 'first-to-market' opportunities. The Canadian Tourism Commission's efforts to promote domestic tourism and encourage Canadians to travel within their own country – especially during periods when the U.S. dollar was particularly strong, and again in the aftermath of September 11, 2001 – is an example of this.

- ➤ International crises: tragedies such as war or health emergencies can have a tremendous and long-lasting impact on global economies.

SOCIETAL FACTORS

While societal and cultural trends take time to unfold, their sheer force and momentum may have significant implications for business owners. Consider the following:

- ➤ *Demographics*: The baby boomer generation in North America has contributed to the rise of leisure travel in recent years. How will this trend affect your market?

  Another example is the X and Y generations. What impact will these generations have on your markets and source of staff for employment? With hospitality organizations traditionally relying on a younger labour force to fill front line positions, what is the impact of the lower number of younger people in today's workforce? What opportunities might there be? How will your business transition and focus differently? How will you manage risks accompanying these social changes?

- ➤ *Psychographics*: Behavioral, lifestyle and psychological factors that impact purchasing patterns (e.g., environmental concerns and 'green products', time-poor affluent people, unstable international situations). The advent of dual income families has had impact on the tourism sector: in this target market, more money is available to spend on travel and tourism, but time can be tight. Shorter, more frequent, getaway vacations have become more common as a result.

➢ *Social changes:*

- The blended family – divorced couples remarrying and blending each other's children into a new family unit.

- The rise of consumerism – the needs of consumers (perceived and real) and the importance in serving them with integrity and honesty. This is particularly critical within the service industries of tourism.

- Dual income families, no children.

- Declining birth rates and impact on labour force availability.

- Increasing life expectancy.

- Increased use of the Internet both as an information source, and as a tool to access services. This has become the primary source of travel information for the consumer. For example, Expedia and TripAdvisor.

➢ *Lifestyle changes:*

- Increasing gender equality.

- Telecommuting and 'hoffices' (home-based offices).

- Retraining.

- Employee mobility to competitors.

- Early/post retirement issues – an aging population unable to retire for economic reasons.

➢ *Environmental awareness:*

- Health and safety issues (aging population and related health care issues).

- Focus on the triple bottom line by companies (Profit, People and the Environment).

- International agreements like the Kyoto Protocol.

- "Green" products.

- Recycling and conservation issues.

- Environmental waste clean up.

- Control of emissions.

- Rise in power of environmentally-focused politicians (e.g., the Green Party).

➢ *Other trends specific to tourism include the following:*

- Increased demand for low-cost airlines.

- Growth in special interest travelers, seeking authentic cultural and learning experiences.

- Growth in "hybrid" consumers, who combine bargains (inexpensive flights, fast food meals) and luxuries (deluxe accommodations, spa treatments) within the same vacation.[7]

- Today's traveler is more demanding, knowledgeable, and experienced.

TECHNOLOGICAL CONSIDERATIONS

It is crucial to follow current technology trends both outside and within your industry segment. Consider Moore's Law, which states that while prices keep constant, the processing power of microchips doubles every 18 months. Certainly in the hospitality sector, the influence of technology has been nothing less than revolutionary in some areas. For example, hotel reservation systems have become highly proficient, allowing for easy tracking of yield management data, occupancy rates, demographic trends, and customer data.

Further, the internet has blown open access to an unlimited customer base from every corner of the globe; for hoteliers in particular, registration with Global Distribution Systems such as Expedia or Travelocity allows for unprecedented opportunities to sell vacant rooms to a global customer base.

According to the Hotel Electronic Distribution Network Association (HEDNA), "in the 1st Quarter of 2004, [North American] GDS booking volumes were up 7.4% over the same period in 2003. Sites owned by IAC Travel, including Expedia, Hotels.com and Hotwire accounted for 11% of the Internet reservations for the 34 [hotel] chains surveyed."[8]

TECHNOLOGY ISSUES TO REVIEW:

➤ The emerging importance of Business-to-Business (B2B) e-commerce. Will your company be an electronic buyer or seller or both? How will this impact existing client and supplier relationships?

➤ How will current technology changes impact your company's operations?

- ◆ Product life cycle (likely shorter).
- ◆ Competition.
- ◆ Ability to forge corporate alliances or joint ventures.
- ◆ Access to international markets.
- ◆ Delivery (just in time) and transportation issues.
- ◆ Potential for process improvements and cost savings.
- ◆ Ability to meet customer needs.
- ◆ Location of labour force.

USEFUL WEB SITES

www.statcan.ca	StatsCanada – latest economic indicators
www.canadatourism.com	Canadian Tourism Commission (CTC)
www.tiac-aitc.ca	Tourism Industry Association of Canada (TIAC)
www.hotelassociation.ca	Hotel Association of Canada (HAC)
www.crfa.ca	Canadian Restaurant and Foodservices Association (CRFA)
www.easidemographics.com	Demographic data for target markets
www.ftc.gov	Federal Trade Commission
www.usdoj.gov	U.S. Department of Justice
www.census.gov	U.S. Census Bureau
www.grantthornton.ca	Grant Thornton LLP
www.destinations.ca	Destinations BC's first choice for jobs in Tourism
www.landings.ca	Tourism Management Hiring Solutions

PROVINCIAL TOURISM DEPARTMENTS:

www.tourism.bc.ca	Tourism British Columbia
www.travelalberta.com	Travel Alberta
www.sasktourism.com	Tourism Saskatchewan
www.travelmanitoba.com	Travel Manitoba
www.ontariotravel.net	Ontario Travel
www.bonjourquebec.com	Quebec Tourism
www.tourismnewbrunswick.ca	Tourism New Brunswick
www.gov.nf.ca/tourism	Newfoundland and Labrador Tourism
www.gov.pe.ca/visitorsguide	Prince Edward Island Tourism
www.touryukon.com	Yukon Tourism
www.nwttravel.nt.ca	Northwest Territories Travel and Tourism
www.nunavuttourism.com	Nunavut Tourism

Endnotes

1   Nickerson, Norma Polovitz, *Snapshots: an introduction to tourism, 3rd Canadian Edition*, Pearson / Prentice Hall, Toronto, 2004, pp. 47.

2   These include: Aboriginal Business Canada, the Aboriginal Business Service Network, several programs offered by the Business Development Bank of Canada, the Canada Business Services Centre, the Canadian Commercial Corporation, the Community Futures Development Corporation, several program offered by Human Resources Development Canada, the National Research Council Industrial Research Assistance Program, the Canadian Tourism Human Resource Council, and the Working Ventures Canadian Fund.

3   Nickerson, pp. 59.

4   *Foodservice Facts 2004.* Canadian Restaurant and Foodservice Association, pp. 20.

5   *Corporate Plan Summary, 2003-2007.* Canadian Tourism Commission.

6   Media Release, June 17, 2004, by the Council of Tourism Associations of BC. (http://www.cotabc.com/documents/AIM%20ATSC%20release%20-%20Final4%20June%2017%202004.pdf)

7   Bourree, Frank, *American Market Rebound? 2004 U.S. Travel Intentions.* In Tourism Monitor Grant Thornton, Spring/Summer 2004, pp. 1.

8   *Partners In Marketing, Electronic Distribution Key Drivers and Trends 2004.* Presented at the Hotel Association of Canada's 2004 12th Annual Conference & Trade Show, 9-10 February 2004, Toronto. (http://www.hotelassociation.ca/news/HEDNA.pps)

Chapter 2
Industry Conditions

Overview

Once you have considered the "big picture" factors that influence the overall external business environment, you should then evaluate the specific implications of this business environment as they relate to the tourism industry. This review is important because the factors, trends and risks that characterize the industry as a whole, can also have a fundamental impact on the performance of your individual tourism business and on the strategic operating and marketing decisions that you make.

In order to guide you through this review process, this section provides suggestions for undertaking both a high-level evaluation of tourism industry conditions as well as a more localized assessment of tourism competitive conditions. It also explains the process for defining the competitive advantages of your business, determining how your business measures up relative to your competitors, and understanding the potential opportunities and threats that could impact both the tourism industry generally as well as your business specifically.

1. Industry Evaluation

In the day-to-day process of running a business, it's easy to lose sight of trends and conditions that may end up having significant operating or market demand impacts on your tourism operation. By the time the effect of these trends and conditions becomes apparent, it may be too late to respond effectively or else you may incur significant time and expense costs in trying to "catch up". For this reason, it is important to regularly take the time to step back a bit and evaluate the industry. Following is a list of some of the factors that should be considered as part of this evaluation process, which should generally be done on a fairly broad basis.

Describe the industry. Consider key industry features such as its size and growth (both historical and projected growth), as well as product trends, market trends, and the pace and influence of technological change and innovation.

How vulnerable is the tourism industry to the PEST factors outlined in Chapter One? For example:

> Macroeconomic conditions? The economic impacts of September 11, 2001 and SARS were felt by many segments of the tourism industry throughout Canada and the world.

> Political, legal and regulatory issues? The introduction of local hotel room taxes, to generate revenue for marketing initiatives, is an example of a regulatory trend that has drawn both support and opposition.

> Environmental concerns and technological trends? In response to "go green" trends, a number of hotel chains have introduced environmental protection policies that have reduced laundry volumes and resulted in some cost savings. The increased use of the Internet to research and book travel has led to a significant shake-out amongst traditional travel agencies.

> Demographic influences? Although you've heard it many times, there is no denying that the aging baby boomer market is having, and will continue to have, a significant impact on leisure travel demand and preferences. At the same time, there are fewer younger people available to fill the traditional service and tourism jobs needed to meet the demands of the baby boomer market.

Consider the life-cycle stage of your specific tourism industry segment. By examining the life-cycle stages of your industry segment, you should be able to pinpoint its present age. For example:

- Early stage?   Cuisine tourism
- Growth?   Spa tourism
- Shake-out?   Group Tour
- Maturity?   Downhill skiing
- Decline?   Traditional travel agencies

Assess "Driving Forces". Driving forces are factors that may result in major future change in the tourism industry and include, for example:

> Internationalization: The growth of Internet use allows even small tourism operators to market their business to potential visitors from around the world.

> Significant changes in the interests and needs of travelers: For example, an increased interest in nature, the environment and learning has led to a significant growth in ecotourism and edutourism products.

> New methods of marketing or distributing tourism products: As noted earlier, the increased use of the Internet to research and book travel means that cyber-sites such as Travelocity and Expedia are replacing travelers' reliance on traditional travel agencies.

> Fundamental changes in government polices or societal attitudes: The formation of the Canadian Tourism Commission in 1995 represented an important political signal that the federal government formally recognized the value and future potential of the tourism industry along with the need to address a serious national travel deficit.

> New technologies that create efficiencies: New technology developments related to reservations and point of sale systems, security, and global distribution systems (e.g. Sabre) have introduced many new efficiencies to the tourism industry.

2. INDUSTRY COMPETITIVE CONDITIONS

Once you have completed a general examination of tourism industry trends and conditions, you should assess the competitive environment within which your tourism business operates. Understanding the nature and intensity of your competition is key to making effective operating and marketing decisions.

One way of assessing competitive forces within your segment of the tourism industry is to use the Five Forces model developed by Michael Porter of the Harvard Business School. This model provides a framework for analyzing the primary competitive forces that are influencing the industry. This framework is illustrated in the following figure and shows the relationship between various companies operating within the tourism industry and various competitive forces.

Figure 2-1

THE INDUSTRY COMPETITIVE ENVIRONMENT

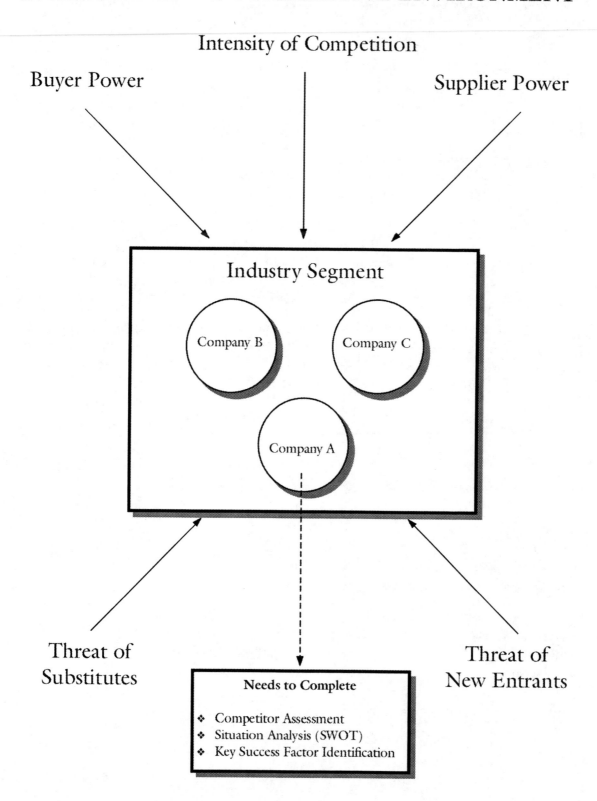

Intensity of Competition

Buyer Power

Supplier Power

Industry Segment

Company B

Company C

Company A

Threat of
Substitutes

Threat of
New Entrants

Needs to Complete

❖ Competitor Assessment
❖ Situation Analysis (SWOT)
❖ Key Success Factor Identification

The Five Forces model uses a series of questions grouped into five categories to help you gauge the relative intensity of the competitive forces facing your tourism industry segment, as follows:

THREAT OF NEW ENTRANTS OR BARRIERS TO ENTRY

➤ Are high levels of capital investment required to enter your industry segment?

➤ Do existing tourism operators have the ability to retaliate against new entrants by using pricing or new product/service strategies?

➤ Do existing operators enjoy economies of scale?

➤ Is brand loyalty a powerful force in this segment?

➤ How difficult is it to obtain the necessary skilled personnel or materials?

➤ How difficult is it to obtain regulatory approvals?

BARGAINING POWER OF CUSTOMERS/VISITORS (BUYER POWER)

➤ How likely is it that customers/visitors will switch to another business?

➤ Do your visitors recognize your tourism product or service as unique?

➤ Can visitors obtain your tourism product or service from multiple suppliers?

BARGAINING POWER OF SUPPLIERS (SUPPLIER POWER)

➤ Are there other potential product or service suppliers?

➤ Do direct labour and purchase costs (cost of goods sold – COGS) have a significant impact on overall operating costs?

THREAT OF SUBSTITUTE PRODUCTS AND SERVICES

➤ How likely or able are visitors to switch to different tourism product or service providers?

➤ Will visitors incur costs when switching to other providers?

INTENSITY OF RIVALRY AMONG EXISTING COMPETITORS

➤ Is the industry segment growing rapidly and accommodating new competitors?

➤ Are there significant product, service and brand identity differences between competitors?

➤ Is the competition local, national or global?

The following table can be used to assess the level of competitive forces facing your tourism business.

Evaluation of Industry Competitive Conditions

	Favorable	Neutral	Unfavorable
Threat of New Entrants	Low	Medium	High
Bargaining Power of Customers	Low	Medium	High
Bargaining Power of Suppliers	Low	Medium	High
Threat of Substitutes	Low	Medium	High
Intensity of Rivalry between Competitors	Low	Medium	High

By using the above table to answer each of the Five Forces questions, you can determine whether competitive forces relative to your business are favourable, neutral or unfavourable.

For example: you determine that the Threat of New Entrants is Low. This would be considered a favourable influence that will allow your business to survive and prosper. However, you also determine that the Bargaining Power of Customers or Visitors is High. This would be considered an unfavourable influence and should lead you to consider strategies for differentiating your product and creating an awareness of value for money.

As illustration of how the Five Forces model could be applied to a specific segment of the tourism industry is provided below.

Evaluation of Industry Competitive Conditions

Bed and Breakfast Industry in Victoria, B.C.

	Favorable	Neutral	Unfavorable
Threat of New Entrants		Medium	
Bargaining Power of Customers			High
Bargaining Power of Suppliers	Low		
Threat of Substitutes			High
Intensity of Rivalry between Competitors	Low		

In Victoria, B.C., the threat of new entrants to the B&B industry is rated as Medium. Although there is a significant barrier to entry due to the capital requirements to start this kind of business, the associated regulatory environment is less complex than in other locales, and therefore favourable. Additionally, although running this kind of business does not require specific education or skills, nonetheless it is a demanding industry to work in over the long-term, and is not suitable for everyone.

The bargaining power of customers or visitors is rated as High. Visitors can choose from numerous B&B operations in the city and switching costs are low. To minimize this threat, operators must develop a focused, targeted marketing plan that reaches their target market in a variety of ways, and highlights the features that differentiates their operation from its competitors.

The bargaining power of suppliers is rated as Low. Standard suppliers of food and linens are numerous in the city, and pricing is relatively consistent across suppliers. In addition, the contribution of Cost of Goods Sold in this industry is lower compared to the fixed costs of assets such as land and buildings.

The threat of substitutes is rated as High. Visitors to Victoria can choose from a variety of accommodation options including independent boutique hotels, large chain hotels, luxury resorts, motels, and even hostels. Again, a way to mitigate this threat could be to offer as unique a product as possible, that customers cannot find elsewhere. For example, Swans Hotel operates a small art gallery out of its premises, and features a rotating sample of works from local and national artists.

Within the Bed and Breakfast industry, the intensity of rivalry amongst competitors is rated as Low; the industry is relatively cooperative and collaborative. Especially in the busy summer season, there are usually enough customers to go around.

Given this analysis, if you are thinking of opening a Bed and Breakfast business in Victoria, you might conclude that you should proceed only if you are able to offer a product that is quite unique from other businesses already in the city. Given the high bargaining power of customers, and the ease of substituting the B&B experience for other accommodation options in the Victoria market, it might also be prudent to purchase an existing business rather than create a new business as a start-up.

3. Competitor Assessment

After reviewing the competitive environment of your industry segment, you need to focus in and assess those businesses that you would consider your direct competitors. The objective of this assessment is to try and determine the factors or influences that have contributed to the relative strength of your industry peers. These factors will vary according to the nature and scale of your tourism operation but could include:

> - Economies of scale
> - Deep pockets (sufficient financial resources to meet working capital requirements and deter new entrants)
> - Superior distribution channels
> - Brand/market image
> - Product and service offerings

While it is not always easy to obtain the following information, these sources can be used to help understand your competition and to keep up with industry segment trends:

> - Your employees. Every wise tourism operator knows that their employees are their strongest asset. They may have current knowledge about your competitors and how you measure up in your industry segment. Ask them!
> - Industry associations and directories. For example, Local Chamber of Commerce directories, accommodation associations, etc.
> - Your customers. Ask your customers how you stack up against your competitors.
> - The Internet. The Internet is becoming your visitors' information source of choice and it should be yours, too. Check out competitors' web sites and online media archives.
> - Strategis. Strategis is Industry Canada's web page to provide business and consumer information.

➤ Financial Securities firms' research reports. Select those firms where analysts are top ranked for a particular industry sector.

➤ Trade publications. Industry trends and new initiatives are regularly featured in trade publications, which are available for almost every segment of the tourism industry.

➤ Trade shows. Check out your competition in the flesh!

➤ Indusry consultants such as Grant Thornton.

4. COMPETITIVE ADVANTAGE

To grow and prosper your tourism business, it is crucial to create and maintain a strong competitive advantage over your competitors. In order to do this, you have to know what your competitive advantage is.

For the tourism industry, competitive advantage can be examined from global, regional, and local perspectives. At the broadest level, all tourism businesses are competing with all other businesses in terms of trying to attract visitors from around the world. To assist in this endeavor, part of the CTC's mandate is to promote Canada internationally as a travel destination. Compared to other countries in today's economic and political climate, Canada offers numerous competitive advantages to travelers, such as safety, accessibility, positive currency exchange rates, and natural beauty.

At the next geographic level, provinces, and even areas within provinces (think of the rivalry between Edmonton and Calgary, for example), also compete against each other for travel market share. The tourism departments of each province and territory highlight the specific travel advantages of their specific area. Competitive advantage at this level is, therefore, largely focused on the particular features of the province or region that might attract visitors. For example, British Columbia's tourism industry cannot compete for visitors interested in Anne of Green Gables or polar bears.

However, it is at the local level that competition becomes most challenging. Once a visitor has arrived at their destination of choice and decides to go out for dinner, his or her choice of a restaurant becomes dependent upon finding a food service outlet that is appealing on a multitude of levels including meal prices, type of food, location, etc. It is at this level that the success or failure of your business becomes highly dependent on its competitive advantage and its ability to attract this potential customer.

In order to evaluate the specific competitive advantages of your business, you need to understand your Key Success Factors (KSFs): the specific attributes of your business that give it a competitive advantage relative to other operations in your industry segment.

Every tourism operator should be able to identify four to five KSFs for their business. For example, does your business enjoy:

> ➢ Cost advantages? Being able to control your operating costs is key to the financial success of most businesses. Therefore, an operator of a franchised restaurant likely benefits from some cost advantages compared to independent food service operations, because of the significant economies of scale associated with being part of a franchise system.

> ➢ Quality advantages? Quality is determined and recognized by your customers. For example, a hotel property on the beach would normally be seen to have a quality advantage over a comparable but landlocked property. In general, travelers are willing to pay more for a quality product or service.

> ➢ Location advantages? Where your tourism business is located can create competitive advantages from both a market and operations perspective. For example, tourism businesses in urban settings typically find it easier to access to skilled labour than businesses in more remote locations. Likewise, the remote location of your business could enhance its market appeal by providing access to unique or appealing tourist experiences.

> ➢ Effective and efficient packaging and market distribution channels? Within the tourism industry, packaging or partnership opportunities can add value to a product offering and increase its market appeal. For example, the air travel/car rental partnership between WestJet Airlines and National Car Rentals, makes transportation easier for travelers and creates marketing efficiencies.

> ➢ A highly skilled workforce? Are your workers helping or hindering your business? Are they friendly or surly with visitors and other staff? Do they go the extra step to make visitors feel welcome and special? Do they have the right skills? Do you operate in a region that offers hospitality education programs? Do not under-estimate the competitive advantage associated with having an appropriately skilled and functional workforce.

> ➢ An advantageous regulatory environment? What kind of impact does the regulatory environment in which you operate have on your tourism business? Think about room taxes, liquor laws, zoning restrictions, and so forth. Support for the tourism industry varies in different areas, and regions that are pro-tourism may have both a more supportive regulatory environment, as well as lobbying bodies that protect the interests of tourism businesses.

5. SITUATION ANALYSIS

The last key step in the industry assessment process is to complete a Situation Analysis. The purpose of a situation analysis is to identify the 'high level' opportunities and threats that could impact your industry segment. In turn, your business strategy should focus on taking advantage of opportunities and addressing or mitigating threats. Consider the following:

Opportunities

- ➤ Are favourable shifts in traveler market preferences taking place?
- ➤ Are new visitor products and/or service offerings available?
- ➤ Are new visitor market segments emerging?
- ➤ Is there potential for new marketing channels?
- ➤ Are favourable changes in the regulatory environment expected?
- ➤ Do you anticipate new uses for existing services or products?
- ➤ Are there opportunities for new partnerships or alliances?

Threats

- ➤ Do you expect adverse changes in visitor market trends?
- ➤ Is exchange rate volatility expected?
- ➤ Could substitute destination/products/service offerings emerge?
- ➤ Are new competitors anticipated?
- ➤ Is a market slowdown forecast?

USEFUL WEB SITES:

www.ceoexpress.com	CEO Express
www.sbfocus.com	Small Business Focus – research materials
www.dnb.ca	Dun & Bradstreet – industry ratios
www.bluebook.ca	Online database search engine – Canadian companies
www.sedar.com	Database on Canadian public companies
www.canadatourism.com	Canadian Tourism Commission (CTC)
www.hotelsmag.com	Hotels Magazine
www.wttc.org	World Travel and Tourism Council (WTTC)
www.worldtravelers.org	World Travelers of America (WTA)
www.tiac-aitc.ca	Tourism Industry Association of Canada (TIAC)
www.bizlink.com/food	Food in Canada, The Voice of the Canadian Food & Beverage Industry

SECTION 2

THE INTERNAL

'SIZE-UP'

CHAPTER 3
THE FINANCIAL EVALUATION

OVERVIEW

This chapter deals with the financial health of your company – a crucial component to your survival and success. The Canadian Tourism Commission recently produced a series of six financial guides for tourism operators. The full series is entitled The ABCs of Financial Performance Measures and Benchmarks for Canada's Tourism Sector. Guide 1: Financial Planning: Key to Maximizing Your Bottom Line offers an introductory explanation of the importance of financial evaluation for all tourism operators that may assist those who are new to financial evaluation. The full series of Guides can be found on the CTC website at: www.canadatourism.com. In this chapter, we will look at six key areas of financial evaluation:

> ➤ Financial Statements

> This section provides an overview of the Balance Sheet, Income Statement, and Statement of Cash Flows, along with a brief summary of the types of financial statement presentations that are available.

> ➤ Financial Goals and Ratio Analysis

> The six key indicators of your corporate financial health are presented. We also demystify ratio analysis and show you how to build an effective diagnostic toolbox.

> ➤ Financial Projections

> An overview of pro forma Balance Sheet, Income, and Cash Flow Statements that forecast your anticipated financial performance in the future.

> Managing 'Cash Drivers'

> Some useful tips to manage your working capital and cash cycles are outlined.

> Breakeven Analysis

> A concise explanation of the relationship between revenue and fixed/variable costs is provided.

> Capital Budgeting Techniques

> An overview of longer term investment decision making is presented.

FINANCIAL STATEMENTS

Financial statements are essential tools that are used to analyze and assess your business performance.

> Lenders require them to expedite loan applications.

> Company owners need them to track financial performance and to determine their financial health.

> Suppliers often want to review them in order to grant credit and to ensure that new clients can pay them.

> Clients may check them to reassure themselves that their key suppliers will be around for awhile.

The following three separate, yet closely interrelated, financial statements will be reviewed:

1. The Balance Sheet: provides a snapshot of a company's financial position at a set point in time.

2. The Income (or Profit and Loss or Operating) Statement: reveals the company's revenue, expenses, and profit performance over a specific period of time.

3. The Cash Flow Statement: indicates how much and by what means cash was generated by the company over a specific time and how it was used.

1. THE BALANCE SHEET

The Balance Sheet lists and totals the assets, liabilities, and owners' equity at the end of an operating period (i.e. December 31st, 2001). The relationship between assets and liabilities is shown by the following formula.

ASSETS – LIABILITIES = OWNERS' EQUITY

Assets: Consist of cash and items you can easily convert into cash (like securities and accounts receivable), and include items you need to make products and provide services (like inventory, equipment, or machinery). Assets on the Balance Sheet are usually listed in order of how quickly each can be converted into cash or liquidity.

Liabilities: Are amounts owed by the company and are usually classified as Current Liabilities (due within one year) or Long-term Liabilities which are listed according to how soon each liability has to be repaid.

Owners or Shareholders equity: Reflects the funds contributed to the company for ownership interest as well as the accumulation of profits or losses derived in the past (Retained Earnings).

An example of a Balance Sheet is shown below:

ABC Company Balance Sheet As of December 31, 2000 (thousands of dollars)		1999		2000	Change
Assets					
Current Assets:					
Cash		$ 4,000		$ 1,800	-$ 2,200
Marketable securities		$ 2,000		$ 2,000	
Accounts receivable		$ 4,000		$ 5,000	$ 1,000
Inventory		$ 4,000		$ 4,600	$ 600
Prepaid expenses		$ 200		$ 200	
Total Current Assets		$ 14,200		$ 13,600	-$ 600
Property, Plant, And Equipment					
Historical cost	$10,000		$12,000		
Less accumulated depreciation	$ 6,000	$ 4,000	$ 6,400	$ 5,600	$ 1,600
Other Assets					
Investment in subsidiary		$ 800		$ 800	
Total Assets		$ 19,000		$ 20,000	$ 1,000
Liabilities & Owners' Equity					
Current Liabilities:					
Accounts payable		$ 600		$ 1,000	$ 400
Accrued expenses		$ 2,600		$ 2,400	-$ 200
Current portion of long-term debt		$ 400		$ 400	
Total Current Liabilities		$ 3,600		$ 3,800	$ 200
Long-term Debt		$ 4,000		$ 3,600	-$ 400
Total Liabilities		$ 7,600		$ 7,400	
Shareholders' Equity:					
Capital Stock	$ 4,000		$ 4,000		
Retained Earnings	$ 7,400	$ 11,400	$ 8,600	$ 12,600	$ 1,200
Total Liabilities & Shareholders Equity		$ 19,000		$ 20,000	$ 1,000

2. INCOME STATEMENT (PROFIT OR LOSS)

> ➤ Indicates how much money the company made or lost over a reporting period.

> ➤ The statement shows revenues generated from selling goods and/or services with the Cost of Goods Sold (COGS), operating expenses, financing costs, and taxes deducted to arrive at a net income figure.

The following statement summarizes the key components:

ABC Company
Income Statement
For the year ending December 31, 2000
(thousands of dollars)

Net Sales		$ 20,000
Cost of goods sold		$ 14,000
Gross Profit		$ 6,000
Operating Expenses:		
Selling	$ 1,200	
Administrative	$ 2,000	
Depreciation	$ 400	$ 3,600
Income from operations		$ 2,400
Interest expense		$ 400
Income before taxes		$ 2,000
Income tax expense		$ 800
Net Income		**$ 1,200**

PROFIT, EARNINGS, AND INCOME:

These terms are often interchanged and for the purposes of this chapter, essentially have the same meaning.

3. THE CASH FLOW STATEMENT (STATEMENT OF CHANGES IN FINANCIAL POSITION)

Remember that revenue is not necessarily received when it is earned and expenses are not always paid when incurred, so it is important to chart the inflow or outflow of cash experienced by the company. The following statement shows the flows of cash (sources and uses) within a company for an operating period of one year. Make note of how the cash flows tie in with the changes to the Balance Sheet and to the Income Statement as outlined on the previous pages.

ABC Company
Statement of Cash Flow
For the year ending December 31, 2000
(thousands of dollars)

Cash flow from Operations:		
Net income	$	1,200
Depreciation (non cash item)	$	400
	$	1,600
Changes in:		
Accounts receivable	$	(1,000)
Inventory	$	(600)
Accounts payable	$	400
Accrued expenses	$	(200)
Net cash provided by Operations	$	200
Cash flows from investing activities:		
Purchase of capital assets	$	(2,000)
Net Cash from financing activities:		
Repayment of long-term debt		(400)
Net cash provided (used)	$	**(2,200)**

TYPES OF FINANCIAL STATEMENTS

While financial statements provide critical information to company owners, the basis of presentation and the source of the information deserve careful consideration.

a) Basis of presentation
Company owners need to ensure that their financial statements are prepared in accordance with Generally Accepted Accounting Principles (GAAP). This process ensures that the financial data is consistently presented, thereby allowing meaningful comparison between time periods.

A key principle called full disclosure compels management to ensure that all liabilities and material facts are presented.

b) The source and integrity of the information
In Canada, you will encounter three types of financial statements that provide different levels of comfort to their readers.

1) *Notice to Reader:*
Essentially a compilation of the company owners' financial records with no verifications or limited investigation completed by the external accountant.

2) *Review Engagement:*
Greater comfort is provided by certain tests and verifications that are completed by the accountant and accompanied by detailed explanatory notes. The resulting financial statements are the most common form of presentation and are usually acceptable to most investors, bankers or suppliers.

3) *Audited Financial Statements:*
These are the most expensive and comprehensive and are normally completed by large private firms, public companies, and government institutions.

The Canadian Tourism Commission Financial Performance series' Guide 2: Profiling Your Financial Statements offers a more detailed, step-by-step discussion of financial statements, using tourism companies as illustrative examples, which may provide additional understanding. The full series of Guides can be found on the CTC website at: www.canadatourism.com.

FINANCIAL GOALS AND RATIO ANALYSIS

OVERVIEW

To effectively assess a company's relative financial health, we present six key indicators that you should consider.

These key indicators are presented along with brief explanations. The financial ratios (diagnostic tests) which are pertinent to each category are also provided.

1. PROFITABILITY AND CASH FLOW

- ➤ Gross Profit

    - ◆ indicates the total margin available to cover operating expenses.

    - ◆ reflects product line pricing decisions and/or the impact of purchases/materials on price levels.

    - ◆ also an indicator of 'margin performance'.

    - ◆ Formula - $\underline{\text{Sales - Cost of Goods Sold}} \times 100 = (\%)$
      Sales

- ➤ Net Profit (The bottom line)

    - ◆ shows after tax profits per $ of sales (%).

    - ◆ below standard performance points to weak sales performance or relatively high costs or both.

    - ◆ also stated as net income or earnings.

    - ◆ Formula - $\underline{\text{Profit After Taxes}} \times 100 = (\%)$
      Sales

- ➤ Return On Equity

    - ◆ measures the rate of return on a shareholders' investment in the company.

    - ◆ does return compensate for risk? (compare to prevailing Government of Canada Bond returns or opportunity costs of other investments).

    - ◆ Formula - $\underline{\text{Profit After Taxes} \times 100} = \%$
      $\text{Total Shareholders Equity}$

> EBITDA

  ♦ defined as Earnings Before Interest, Taxes, Depreciation, and Amortization.

  ♦ indicates the effective cash flow generated by a company on an annual basis.

  ♦ there is a more complex and sophisticated step that uses a 'free cash flow' measurement. This calculates the company's annual cash flows by including changes in Accounts Receivable, Inventory and Accounts Payable (working capital items). Their use and application is beyond the scope of this text.

  ♦ the market value of a firm is sometimes estimated using EBITDA (e.g. 4 times EBITDA.)

2. LIQUIDITY

Liquidity is defined as the ability to meet short-term obligations and measures the relationship between current assets and current liabilities.

> Working Capital

> reveals the balance between liquid assets and claims of short-term creditors.

> is derived by deducting current liabilities from current assets.

> Current Ratio Formula = $\dfrac{\text{Current Assets}}{\text{Current Liabilities}}$

> A current ratio over 1.5:1 is normally a positive indicator although the nature and relative liquidity of the current assets needs to be considered.

> The Quick Ratio demonstrates a firm's ability to pay off short-term obligations without reliance on the need to sell inventory.

> Formula - $\dfrac{\text{Current Assets - Inventory}}{\text{Current Liabilities}}$

Figure 3-1 (below) demonstrates the relationship between a company's "net" working capital and the other components of the Balance Sheet.

Figure 3-1

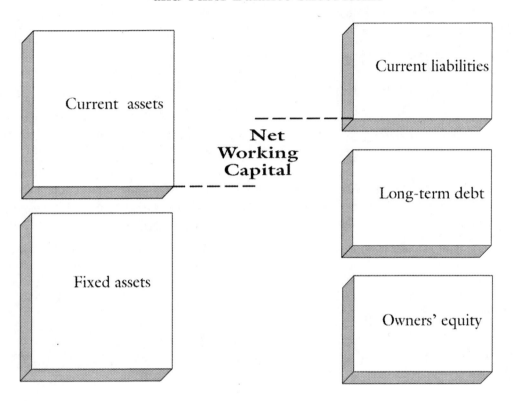

Relationship between Working Capital and other Balance Sheet items

3. STABILITY

➢ Debt to Equity Ratio

◆ measures the relationship between debt and equity.

◆ indicates the extent of funds provided by creditors (debt) and company owners (equity).

◆ leverage varies from industry to industry – under 2.5:1 is normally a reasonable comfort zone.

♦ Formula -   Total Liabilities
                     Total Equity

Note: Intangible assets such as patents, goodwill, etc., should be deducted from the Equity number.

Shareholder loans are sometimes 'subrogated' or 'postponed' to the primary debt holder, which allows this item to be removed from the Liabilities section and added back to Equity thus improving the Debt to Equity ratio.

➤ Total Debt/EBITDA

   ♦ measures the relationship between debt and cash flow – the time frame over which debt is retired from cash flow.

   ♦ Formula -   Total Liabilities
                        EBITDA

Note: The EBITDA number is often trimmed back by deducting annual capital expenditures (abbreviated as 'capex') that reoccur on a regular basis. This provides a more accurate indication of cash generation for the year period.

4. DEBT SERVICE

The ability of a company to pay interest and principal on its debt obligations is a key indicator of financial health.

➤ Interest Coverage

   ♦ demonstrates the extent that annual cash flow covers debt interest obligations.

   ♦ Formula -   EBITDA
                        Annual Interest

➤ Debt Service Coverage

   ♦ reveals the extent that annual cash flows cover annual required debt payments (principal and interest).

   ♦ Formula -   EBITDA
                     Annual Principal and Interest payments

Note: Annual capital expenditures can also be deducted from the EBITDA number to derive a more accurate cash generation figure.

5. EFFICIENCY

These formulas measure the effective management of working capital items (Accounts Receivable, Inventory, Accounts Payable).

- ➤ Accounts Receivable Collection

  - ◆ Formula - $$\frac{\text{Accounts Receivable x 365}}{\text{Sales}}$$

  - ◆ measures the average time (number of days) it takes the business to collect sales made on credit terms.

  - ◆ a weak ratio – more than 60 days – points to suspect collection procedures, slow billing or poor credit judgment.

- ➤ Inventory Turnover

  - ◆ Formula - $$\frac{\text{Cost of Goods Sold}}{\text{Average Inventory}}$$

  - ◆ indicates whether the firm has excessive or inadequate inventories (industry comparisons are required to accurately assess the numbers).

  - ◆ slow inventory turnover may point to acceptance of too many quantity discounts or slow-moving product lines.

- ➤ Accounts Payable Settlement

  - ◆ Formula - $$\frac{\text{Accounts Payable x 365}}{\text{Annual Purchases}}$$

  - ◆ indicates the average time (number of days) taken to settle accounts with creditors and suppliers.

  - ◆ points to consider: - are extended payment terms negotiable?
    - are alternative credit sources available?
    - are early payment discounts available?

6. GROWTH

These percentages measure the extent and pace of expansion and are usually calculated for Sales, Net Profits, Assets, Debt and Equity.

To assess a company's growth strategy, the following issues must be considered:

➤ What future sales volumes are anticipated as the company expands its product lines and markets?

➤ What levels of profitability and cash generation are forecast and are they sustainable?

➤ What level of bank operating credit is required? Are there seasonal financing needs?

➤ What level of long-term debt is required to finance future capital expenditures and will the company be able to service and repay its increased debt load?

➤ What are the working capital implications of a particular growth strategy and will higher levels of accounts receivable and/or inventories result (uses of cash)?

➤ Can extended payment terms be negotiated with suppliers (sources of cash)?

➤ Can the company raise additional equity? If equity is raised is there a market for minority shares and what percentage ownership stake would be sold and at what price?

➤ Does the company have assets (i.e. real estate) that could be sold or refinanced to raise additional funds?

SOME CONCLUDING COMMENTS ABOUT FINANCIAL RATIOS

➤ Ratio analysis allows you to measure comparative performance over selected time periods. For example, by comparing the following current ratio, a specific, improving trend can be identified:

2002	2003	2004
2.1	2.4	2.6

It is important to ensure that the same time periods and time of year are used (e.g. comparing the twelve month period ended December 31st, 2004 to December 31st, 2005).

➤ Performance in relation to competitor firms can be assessed by obtaining Industry comparables from Dun & Bradstreet and Robert Morris and Associates (RMA) publications.

Example – Company ABC current ratio fiscal 2004 = 1.2 (weaker)
Industry comparable ratio same year   = 1.8

The Canadian Tourism Commission Financial Performance series' Guide 3: Financial Performance Measures and Benchmarks for Canada's Tourism Operators offers a more detailed, step-by-step discussion of financial analysis using ratios, and uses tourism companies as illustrative examples, which may provide additional understanding.

Guide 6: Industry Financial Averages and Benchmarks for Canada's Tourism Operators details some industry statistics for a variety of tourism groups. The full series of Guides can be found on the CTC website at: www.canadatourism.com.

MANAGING CASH DRIVERS

OVERVIEW

Effective management of short-term assets (cash, accounts receivable, inventories) and short-term sources of financing (accounts payable, bank operating lines) is an important component of the financial evaluation.

Cash drivers are those management strategies that result in accelerated generation and accumulation of cash resources as part of the working capital cycle.

Before detailing the three primary cash drivers, a key distinction needs to be made between net income (or profit or earnings) and net cash flow.

> ➤ net income equals the difference between revenues and expenses.

> ➤ net cash flow equals the difference between cash inflows and outflows.

These will invariably be different, reflecting:

1. the uneven timing of cash disbursements and the accounting treatment of them.

2. the uneven timing of sales revenues and cash receipts due to delays in account receivable collection.

Due to these timing differences, a company may achieve a strong net profit performance (paper profit) and yet experience a serious cash flow shortfall due to negative cash flows. This section illustrates how a company can improve its net cash flow performance by employing selective cash driver strategies.

Three Primary Cash Drivers

1. Improved Accounts Receivable Collection

> Practicing astute credit management

Establish credit limits for each customer category and use banks or agencies for credit reports. Where appropriate, charge interest on overdue accounts and consider accepting VISA / MasterCard (as opposing to extending credit which may lead to protected repayment).

> Effective Invoicing

Issue statements at least monthly and ensure that invoices are submitted on the same day goods are shipped. Negotiate front end payments for custom orders.

> Careful Monitoring

Age receivables by current, 30, 60, and over 90-day categories and place overdue accounts on Cash on Delivery (COD). Monitor and contact overdue accounts on a regular basis.

> Prompt Collection

Establish a formal credit granting and collection policy, including litigation procedures. Wherever possible, negotiate personal guarantees for new and overdue accounts.

2. Defined Accounts Payable Settlement

> Age payables into Current, 30 days, 60 days and over 90-day categories.

> Extend terms with key suppliers, especially to mirror seasonal cash needs. However, if attractive early payment discounts are offered, take advantage of them.

3. Maximize Inventory Turnover

> Return or sell off outdated or obsolete merchandise.

> Determine the number of times your major product lines turn each year. How does this compare to industry averages? The faster the inventory turnover, the greater the cash flow.

> Are shrinkage control procedures in place (to guard against goods slipping out of the back door)?

> Are re-order policies in place based on past inventory levels and target turnover numbers?

> Are the 'costs' of carrying inventory known (i.e. interest and handling costs)?

> Do you have alternative sources of supply (i.e. improved delivery terms)?

OTHER CASH DRIVER STRATEGIES

> Increases in property values (appraisal values versus net book value on the Balance Sheet) may allow refinancing and generate surplus cash (working capital) to finance expansion.

> Consider leasing out under-utilized assets to third parties.

> Borrow short term for short term needs, and borrow long term for longer term needs. Match the maximum amortization of the loan with the expected useful life of the asset.

FINANCIAL PROJECTIONS

OVERVIEW

Up to this point, historical financial information has allowed us to diagnose financial health and performance. An equally important element of the evaluation process is the completion of financial forecasts; in essence, the creation of a financial road map that enables company management to foresee where they are going. This process is particularly important if you are seeking increased bank financing or additional sources of equity. The following section details three key documents that comprise a comprehensive financial forecast:

1. Pro Forma (Projected) Income Statements

2. Projected Balance Sheet

3. Cash Flow Budget

1. PRO FORMA INCOME STATEMENTS

The process:

- ➤ Should cover three to five years into the future.

- ➤ The first two years should include complete quarterly income projections, thereafter annually.

- ➤ Projected revenues should be based on historical and anticipated sales performance.

- ➤ The revenue forecast should be derived from either:

- ➤ market size *multiplied by* estimated % market share *multiplied by* estimated growth rate

or

- ➤ *percentage growth* based on historical performance (i.e. 10% sales growth over the next three years, etc.)

Note: Industry data on market size and growth can reveal how your marketplace is changing as opposed to reliance on your own internal numbers.

- ➤ *Cost of Goods Sold (COGS)* forecast should be based on prevailing industry gross profit margins.

- ➤ *Sales, General and Administration (SGA)* expenses represent company overhead. If revenues are forecast to grow beyond a fixed or relevant range, use an SGA to Revenue ratio to ensure support costs grow in tandem with revenues.

- ➤ *Interest Expense* should be based on forecast levels of long-term financing.

- ➤ *Taxes and Depreciation* forecasts would be based on prevailing tax rates and depreciation allowances.

2. PROJECTED BALANCE SHEET

The process:

- ➤ Three-year outlook: derived from historic ratio analysis and your pro forma Income Statement.

- ➤ Projected Accounts Receivable, Inventory, and Accounts Payable: can be derived from historic ratios and forecast revenues/costs/purchases.

- ➤ Fixed Assets: need to reflect any future significant capital expenditures in the future.

➤ Equity: would reflect any new source of capital and ongoing buildup of retained earnings from forecast net profits (after dividend payout).

➤ Balancing Item: will be either cash or bank operating debt.

Note: It is crucial to document any assumptions regarding the financial ratios.

3. CASH FLOW BUDGET

Will project up to three years out, with the first year calculated on a monthly basis. This process highlights the importance of timing differences in cash receipts and disbursements.

Cash In

➤ Utilize the Projected Income Statement and convert revenue forecasts into cash receipts by month.

➤ Review the Account Receivable listing to determine actual payment terms taken (i.e., 20% of receivables paid in 90 days. Therefore – 20% of January sales are not received until April.)

➤ Other cash receipts would include:

  ◆ supplier rebates.

  ◆ new bank loans.

  ◆ cash injections from new shareholders.

Cash Out

➤ Three main items

  ◆ Overhead expenses: fixed costs like rent, salaries, heat and power.

  ◆ Cash outlays for purchases (inventory) and for direct labor.

  ◆ Intermittent expenses: loan payments, capex, dividends, tax payments.

Remember:

➤ Assembly of the 'cash in' and 'cash out' data allows the completion of a 12 month cash flow forecast which determines the cash position on a monthly basis and resultant short term borrowing or investment requirements.

➤ Clearly document assumptions.

➤ Contrast to actual performance thereby highlighting the impact of your cash driver performance.

> ➤ The cash flow budget is an effective early warning system especially when negative variances between actual and forecast month-end cash positions emerge.

> ➤ It also indicates to a bank or investor that you understand the operations and cash drivers for your business. Month by month presentation is crucial, enabling you to react quickly to shortfalls or significant variances.

A Note on Sensitivity Analysis (also known as 'what-if' analysis or 'stress testing'):

Spreadsheet software allows certain key assumptions (sales growth, gross profit margin, account receivable collection, etc.) to be altered.

Different scenarios can then be generated and presented on a best case/ expected case/ worst case basis, usually over the first year period.

Example:

A hotel is planning to expand operations by constructing a new wing and doubling the available number of hotel rooms. To secure the necessary construction and long term financing, a series of financial projections are prepared with different scenarios presented as to percentage occupancy, average room rates and variable costs.

The lenders can also apply their own sensitivity analysis to the scenarios and calculate a breakeven point versus debt service requirements; i.e., term loan payments are covered at 1.25 times when a 65% occupancy and a 25% drop in average room rates is simulated. The lender then has to consider if this is a reasonable worst case scenario.

The Canadian Tourism Commission Financial Performance series' Guide 5: Linking Your Financial Performance Measures to Your Business Plan offers a more detailed, step-by-step discussion of financial projections, using tourism companies as illustrative examples, which may provide additional understanding. The full series of Guides can be found on the CTC website at: www.canadatourism.com.

BREAKEVEN ANALYSIS

All organizations incur various costs in order to operate. Generally those costs can be broken down into two categories, fixed costs and variable costs.

Fixed costs: are costs that, in total, remain much the same over some relevant range of activity levels. For example, office rent will stay the same over the year no matter what level of service provided. Additional examples of fixed costs include salaries (as distinct from wages), property taxes, depreciation expenses, and lease costs.

Variable costs: are costs that vary with activity volume changes. These costs can generally be expressed as cost per unit or as a percentage of revenue.

Example: It takes a certain amount of dollars worth of materials (paper, ink, labour wages) to produce a book. If the variable cost of producing a book is $10, a print run of 100 books would incur variable costs of $1,000 while a run of 1,000 books would incur variable costs of $10,000.

Some costs can be semi-variable, or semi-fixed.

Example: If a retail outlet in a shopping mall pays $1,000 per month rent plus 5% of monthly gross sales, the $1,000 is fixed and 5% of each month's sales amount paid is variable. Electricity costs and a salary plus 'commissions' compensation plan are other examples of semi-variable costs.

Breakeven analysis is a managerial technique that separates costs into fixed and variable components. At a certain level of activity, revenues are equal to the total costs, fixed plus variable. At that level of activity, the organization is at its breakeven point. It has covered all its costs but has not made a profit or surplus.

Exhibit 1 provides a graphical view of breakeven analysis and indicates the breakeven point:

BREAK-EVEN CHART

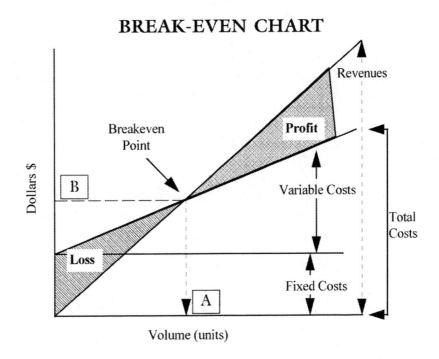

The total fixed costs are fixed over a range of activity volume (units), as indicated by the horizontal line. In addition, each unit sold incurs a variable cost. As volume increases, the total variable costs increase. *The breakeven point is where total revenues equal total costs and is indicated by the point where the revenues line intersects with the total costs line.*

Point A at the bottom of the graph shows the volume level in activity units required to be sold in order to break even.

Point B indicates the dollar amount of revenues required to break even. If the number of units sold exceeds the volume at the breakeven point, a profit or surplus is generated. Alternatively, if the number of units fails to meet the breakeven volume, a loss or deficit occurs.

CONTRIBUTION ANALYSIS

Contribution margin is the amount left over from an activity unit's sale after covering its variable cost. This remaining contribution then goes to cover fixed costs. Therefore, selling price (SP) minus unit variable cost (UVC) equals unit contribution margin (UCM).

Example: If a book is sold for $100 and has a variable cost of $60, the difference of $40 is the unit contribution margin (UCM) available to cover total fixed costs.

If total fixed costs are $10,000, it will take $10,000 divided by the $40 UCM or 250 books to break even. Each and every book sold contributes $40 towards fixed costs. If more than 250 books are sold, each book sold over the 250 breakeven volume, contributes $40 to profit (surplus). Thus if 300 books are sold, the organization has a profit (surplus) of $2,000 ($40 UCM x 50 units over breakeven).

Understanding this concept allows us to change any of the items and assess the impact.

For example, if we thought that variable costs would rise to $65 and we wanted to earn a profit (surplus) of $4,000, we can easily calculate the impact:

SP	$100
UVC	65
UCM	35

➤ Fixed costs + desired profit = $14,000 ($10,000 + $4,000).

➤ $14,000/$35 = 400 books need to be sold to meet our objective.

➤ This translates into $40,000 in revenues (400 books x $100 selling price).

Another approach is on a percentage basis. The UCM is 35% of the SP. By dividing the amount required to be covered ($14,000) by .35 we arrive at the required $40,000 figure.

KEY POINTS

> ➤ The lower the breakeven point, the less vulnerable the firm to unexpected cost increases.

> ➤ The more costs that can be made 'variable' (i.e. occur only once a sale is made) the better.

> ➤ Strive to keep contribution (gross profit) margin high and breakeven point low.

> ➤ Minimize fixed costs.

CAPITAL BUDGETING

Capital budgeting allows a company owner to make financial decisions about long-term investments. Some examples of capital budgeting decisions are:

> ➤ Replacement of company's fleet of vehicles with new models.

> ➤ Development of a new product line that will require extensive R&D and commercialization.

> ➤ Purchase of land parcel and the construction of a new commercial building.

> ➤ Purchase of manufacturing and/or computer equipment.

KEY QUESTION

"Do the future benefits from the investment exceed the costs of making the investment?"

Three different techniques can be used to determine the future benefits with each one answering a specific question.

1. ACCOUNTING RETURN ON INVESTMENT

Question: What average dollar profits are generated per average investment dollar?

Calculation:
$$\frac{\text{Average annual after tax profit per year}}{\text{Average book value of investment}} = \%$$

Example:

New equipment costs $20,000, depreciated over four years to final year (zero salvage value). Average net book value is $10,000.

Expected after tax profits	Year	After tax profit
	1	$2,000
	2	$4,000
	3	$5,000
	4	$6,000

Average expected profits over the four-year period = $4,250

Accounting return on investment = $\dfrac{\$4,250}{\$10,000}$ = 42.5%

SHORTCOMINGS

➤ Based on accounting profits rather than actual cash flows.

➤ Ignores the time value of money.

➤ Company owners' minimum acceptable return (hurdle rate) needs to be established in order to determine acceptance or rejection of the project.

2. PAY BACK PERIOD

Question: How long will it take to recover the original investment?

Calculation: New equipment costs $45,000 with an expected life of 10 years and is depreciated on a straight-line basis at $4,500 per year.

Expected After Tax Cash Flows

Year	After Tax Profit	Depreciation	After Tax Cash Flow
1 to 2	$3,000	+ $4,500	= $7,500
3 to 6	$6,000	+ $4,500	= $10,500
7 to 10	$7,500	+ $4,500	= $11,000

The pay back period will be approximately 4.9 years and is derived by allocating the cumulative annual cash flows against the original $45,000 investment.

STRENGTHS:

➢ Does give an indication of risk – the longer the pay back period, the greater the risk.

WEAKNESSES:

➢ Does not consider the time value of money

➢ Does not consider financial impact of cash flows received after pay back period.

3. DISCOUNTED CASH FLOW

Question: How does the present value of future benefits arising from the investment compare with the present-day cost of the investment?

Discount Cash Flow (DCF) techniques are complex. Two analytical methods can be utilized.

NET PRESENT VALUE (NPV)

The original cash outlay is compared to the value of future cash flows discounted back to the present using a predetermined rate of return (discount rate). If the NPV is positive, then the project is acceptable.

INTERNAL RATE OF RETURN (IRR)

The rate of return that is derived where the present value of the cost of the investment equals the present value of future cash flows.

The Canadian Tourism Commission Financial Performance series' Guide 4: Decision Making Tools for Canada's Tourism Operators offers a more detailed, step-by-step discussion of breakeven analysis and capital budgeting, using tourism companies as illustrative examples, which may provide additional understanding. The full series of Guides can be found on the CTC website at: www.canadatourism.com.

FINANCIAL EVALUATION FOR THE HOSPITALITY INDUSTRY

Hotel operators regularly use the Uniform System of Accounts for Hotels in their tracking and reporting procedures. Some of the terms used in the common system of accounts are as follows:

ROOMS DEPARTMENT

Departmental Revenue

> *Room Sales:* This category includes revenue from guest accommodations rented on a part-day, full-day or longer basis. The figures are net of any sales taxes and service charges paid to employees. Revenue from public rooms ordinarily used for food and beverage service are not included in room sales.

Departmental Expenses

> *Payroll and Related Expenses:* This category includes salaries and wages of rooms department personnel. Also included are employee benefits such as payroll taxes, social insurance, vacation pay, incentive pay, severance pay, bonuses, employee meals, awards, social activities and pensions.

> *Other Expenses:* This category represents expenses other than rooms payroll as defined above, such as room cleaning supplies, contract cleaning, guest supplies, laundry, dry cleaning, linen, reservation expenses, paper supplies, travel agents' commissions, guest transportation, uniforms, credit card discounts and reservation services.

FOOD AND BEVERAGE DEPARTMENT

Departmental Revenue

> ➤ *Food Sales:* This category includes revenue derived from the sale of food (including coffee, milk, tea, juices and soft drinks) through restaurants, lounges (if food is sold), room service, banquets and off-site catering (if applicable).

> ➤ *Beverage Sales:* This category includes revenue from the sale of wine, spirits, liqueurs, juices, beers, ales, mineral waters, and soft drinks used in the preparation of mixed drinks. Beverage sales also include sales of alcoholic beverages for consumption off the premises (if applicable).

Departmental Cost Of Sales

> ➤ *Cost of Food Sales:* This category includes the cost of food served to guests, together with transportation, storage and delivery charges, at the gross invoice price less trade discounts. Commissary and stewards' sales should be credited from these costs. Employee meal costs are charged to the appropriate department and do not constitute a part of the cost of food sold.

> ➤ *Cost of Beverage Sales:* This category represents the cost of wines, spirits, juices, liqueurs, beers, ales, mineral waters and soft drinks and all other beverages used in the preparation of mixed drinks, at the gross invoice price less trade discounts, plus import duties, transportation and delivery charges. Employee beverage costs are charged to the appropriate department and do not constitute a part of the cost of beverages sold. Commissary, stewards' sales, deposit refunds and sales of empty bottles should be credited to these costs.

Departmental Expenses

> ➤ *Payroll and Related Expenses:* This category includes salaries and wages of food and beverage department personnel (purchasing, receiving, storage, preparation, service, dishwashing, cashiers, and control). Also included are all benefits, such as payroll taxes, social insurance, vacation pay, incentive pay, severance pay, bonuses, meals, awards, social activities and pensions.

> ➤ *Other Expenses:* This category includes items such as china and glassware, cutlery, cleaning supplies, contract cleaning, decorations, guest supplies, laundry, linen, music and entertainment, licenses, menus, beverage lists and uniforms.

Telephone Department

> ➤ *Departmental Revenue:* This category includes revenue derived from the use of telephone facilities by guests, divided into local calls, long-distance calls, service charges and commissions received from pay stations. This category

should not be credited with any amounts for telephone services used by management or other departments of the hotel.

Departmental Cost Of Sales

➤ *Cost of Calls:* This expense includes the total amount billed by the telephone companies for local calls and long-distance calls through the switchboard. The cost of automatic internal communication systems should not be charged to this category but should be included in administrative and general expenses.

Departmental Expenses

➤ *Payroll and Related Expenses:* This category includes salaries and wages of telephone department personnel. Also included are employee benefits such as payroll taxes, social insurance, vacation pay, incentive pay, severance pay, bonuses, employee meals, awards, social activities and pensions.

➤ *Other Expenses:* This category includes items such as the cost of printed forms, service manuals, telephone vouchers, message envelopes, telephone directory covers, stationery and office supplies.

MINOR OPERATED DEPARTMENTS

Minor Operated Departmental Revenue

➤ This category includes revenue from guest laundry, garage and valet services. It also includes income from pool club memberships and other minor operated departments such as gift shop, confectionary, spa, art gallery or ecotour sales.

Minor Operated Cost of Sales

➤ This category represents the cost of laundry and valet sales and any other minor operated departmental sales.

Minor Operated Departmental Expenses

➤ *Payroll and Related Expenses:* This category includes salaries and wages of minor operated departments' personnel including guest laundry, valet, garage and pool. Also included are all benefits such as payroll taxes, social insurance, vacation pay, incentive pay, severance pay, bonuses, meals, awards, social activities and pensions. House laundry and employee cafeteria payrolls are not included as they are allocated t the various departments.

➤ *Other Expenses:* This category includes items such as laundry and pool supplies.

Rentals and Other Income

➤ This category includes all income from rental of stores and showcases, profit on foreign exchange, interest income, concession income and other income such as commissions from auto rentals, garage, parking lots and salvage.

UNDISTRIBUTED OPERATING EXPENSES

Administrative and General

➤ *Payroll and Related Expenses:* This category includes salaries and wages of personnel in the administrative and general department, including the manager's office, the accounting office, the credit office, security and night auditors. Also included are all benefits, such as vacation pay, bonuses, meals, awards, social activities and pensions.

➤ *Other Expenses:* This category includes expenses incurred from bad debts, credit card commissions, data processing services, general insurance, licenses and dues, operating supplies, professional fees, security services, travel and entertainment and other related miscellaneous expenses.

Marketing

➤ *Payroll and Related Expenses:* This category includes salaries and wages of marketing department personnel, including personnel in sales, reservations, advertising and other marketing activities. Also included are all benefits such as vacation pay, incentive pay, severance pay, bonuses, meals, awards, social activities and pensions.

➤ *Other Expenses:* This category includes advertising, publicity, franchise fees and other promotional expenses.

Energy

➤ This category includes the cost of fuel, electrical current and water.

Property Operation and Maintenance

➤ *Payroll and Related Expenses:* This category includes salaries and wages of property operation and maintenance department personnel. Also included are all benefits such as vacation pay, incentive pay, severance pay, bonuses, meals, awards, social activities and pensions.

➤ *Other Expenses:* This category includes the cost of materials used in repairing equipment, the exterior and interior of the building (floors, walls, doors, furniture, etc.), grounds and landscaping, painting and decorating, the removal of waste matter and other related expenses.

Management Fees

➤ This category includes fees charged by a management organization for management service or supervision.

FIXED CHARGES

Rent

➤ If the hotel property is leased, this account should be charged with the amount of the rental of the hotel property.

Building and Contents Insurance

➤ The cost of insuring the hotel building and contents against damage or destruction by fire, weather, sprinkler leakage, boiler explosion, plate glass breakage or any other cause.

Property and Business Taxes

➤ This account includes real estate taxes, business taxes, utility taxes and taxes other than income and payroll.

STANDARD INDUSTRY RATIOS

Rate of Occupancy: The percentage of occupancy is the ratio of total occupied rooms to total available rooms.

Average room rate: The average room rate is defined as room sales divided by the total number of rooms occupied.

Food and Beverage Department: Ratios to departmental sales in the food and beverage department are based on total food and beverage sales. The single exception is cost of sales. Cost of food sold is expressed as a percentage of food sales. Similarly, the cost of beverages sold is expressed as a percentage of beverage sales

Staying informed about national trends in operating revenues and expenses can help hotel operators understand their own performance in relation to industry averages. The following is an example of a hotel operating statement, formatted using the Uniform System of Accounts for Hotels:

Figure 3-2

Example Full Service Hotel
Statement of Revenues and Expenses

Rooms		
Number of rooms	200	
Average Room Rate	$ 129.00	
Occupancy	65%	
Room Nights Available	73,000	
Room Nights Sold	47,450	

	Year ended Dec 31	% of Revenue	$ per Available Room
Revenues			
Rooms (Figure 3-3)	$ 6,121,000	65.6%	$ 30,605
Food (Figure 3-3)	2,000,000	21.4%	10,000
Beverage (Figure 3-3)	500,000	5.4%	2,500
Telecommunications	150,000	1.6%	750
Other operating income	340,000	3.6%	1,700
Rentals and other income	220,000	2.4%	1,100
	9,331,000	100.0%	46,655
Departmental expenses			
Rooms (Figure 3-3)	1,665,000	27.2%	8,325
Food and beverage (Figure 3-3)	2,058,000	82.3%	10,290
Telecommunications	87,000	58.1%	435
Other operating departments	239,000	70.3%	1,195
	4,049,000	43.4%	20,245
Departmental gross profit	5,282,000	56.6%	26,410
Undistributed expenses (Figure 3-4)			
Administration and general	727,700	7.8%	3,639
Marketing	513,300	5.5%	2,567
Energy expenses	354,700	3.8%	1,774
Maintenance	401,300	4.3%	2,007
	1,997,000	21.4%	9,987
Income before fixed charges	3,285,000	35.2%	16,423
Fixed expenses			
Property and business taxes	513,200	5.5%	2,566
Insurance	112,000	1.2%	560
	625,200	6.7%	3,126
Income before other fixed charges	$ 2,659,800	28.5%	$ 13,297

Figure 3-3

Example Full Service Hotel
Departmental Revenues and Expenses

Rooms Operations

	Year ended Dec 31	% of Revenue
Revenues		
Room sales	$ 6,121,000	100.0%
Departmental expenses		
Wages & benefits	1,077,000	17.6%
Laundry, linen and guest supplies	165,000	2.7%
Commissions and reservation expenses	184,000	3.0%
Operating supplies and other expenses	239,000	3.9%
Total departmental expense	1,665,000	27.2%
Departmental net income	$ 4,456,000	72.8%

Food and Beverage Operations

	Year ended Dec 31	% of Revenue
Sales		
Food	$ 2,000,000	80.0%
Beverage	500,000	20.0%
Total sales	2,500,000	100.0%
Cost of sales		
Food	646,000	32.3%
Beverage	152,000	30.4%
Total cost of sales	798,000	31.9%
Gross margin	1,702,000	68.1%
Other income	270,000	10.8%
Gross profit and other income	1,972,000	78.9%
Operating expenses		
Wages & benefits	1,265,000	50.6%
Laundry and dry cleaning	30,000	1.2%
China, glassware, sliver, linen	32,500	1.3%
Contract cleaning	20,000	0.8%
Operating supplies and other	182,500	7.3%
Total operating expenses	1,530,000	61.2%
Total departmental expense (net of other income)	2,058,000	82.3%
Departmental net income	$ 442,000	17.7%

THE FINANCIAL EVALUATION 63

Figure 3-4

Example Full Service Hotel
Undistributed Expenses

Undistributed expenses	Year ended Dec 31	% of Total Revenues
Administration and general		
Payroll and related expenses	$ 373,200	4.0%
Bad debts	9,300	0.1%
Credit card discounts	140,000	1.5%
Data processing	9,300	0.1%
Licences and dues	9,300	0.1%
Office supplies	42,000	0.5%
Professional fees	23,300	0.3%
Security	9,300	0.1%
Travel and entertainment	18,700	0.2%
Other	93,300	1.0%
	727,700	7.8%
Marketing		
Payroll and related expenses	168,000	1.8%
Sales expenses	56,000	0.6%
Advertising and promotion	102,600	1.1%
Franchise fees	168,000	1.8%
Other	18,700	0.2%
	513,300	5.5%
Property operation and maintenance		
Payroll and related expenses	168,000	1.8%
Other	233,300	2.5%
	401,300	4.3%
Energy expenses		
Fuel	112,000	1.2%
Electricity	168,000	1.8%
Water	56,000	0.6%
Other	18,700	0.2%
	354,700	3.8%
Total Undistributed Expenses	$ 1,997,000	21.4%

USEFUL WEB SITES

www.rmahq.org	RMA annual statement studies providing comparative financial ratio data. Note: these reports can also be accessed through your local commercial banker.
www.chipsbooks.com/unilodg.htm	Home page for CHIPS (Culinary and Hospitality Industry Publications Services), through which copies of the Uniform System of Accounts for Hotels can be ordered.

CHAPTER 4
MARKETING STRATEGY

OVERVIEW

There tends to be much confusion about what 'marketing' is. Many business people think that marketing is selling, or that it can be summarized by the 4 P's of marketing – price, product, promotion and place (distribution). While these items are encompassed by marketing, there is much more to this critical area of business. For the tourism sector, "…the marketing function in service businesses finds itself closely interrelated with – and dependent upon – the procedures, personnel, and facilities managed by the operations function."[1] Tourism operators are unique in that they sell experiences, services and time. The "product" is generally expensive, intangible, highly perishable (i.e., if you do not sell the hotel room that night, you will never have the chance to recover that lost revenue), and in many cases, seasonal. With such unique features, special attention must be paid to the activities and avenues chosen to market tourism products, to overcome these limitations as much as possible.

OUR DEFINITION:

Marketing is a series of activities which involve analysis of the marketplace, development of a market-driven strategy, and execution of that strategy. These activities allow a company to provide targeted customers with a portfolio of products and services that add value and meet unfulfilled customer needs.

This chapter addresses the following topics:

1. Market analysis

2. Market strategy development

3. Market strategy execution

1. MARKET ANALYSIS

Completion of a careful market analysis is the crucial first stage in developing a comprehensive marketing strategy. A tourism market analysis process involves the following five steps:

A. Segment analysis

B. Competitor evaluation

C. Distribution analysis

D. Sustainable competitive advantage review

E. Unmet customer needs assessment

A. SEGMENT ANALYSIS

Although there are certainly unique challenges in marketing tourism products that are perishable, intangible, and seasonal, nonetheless, these products are sought by a very wide range of diverse customers with unique interests and needs. Target marketing, based upon careful market segmentation – dividing the overall market into groups of people who share similar characteristics or desires – allows for more efficient marketing strategies.

For example, a successful application of market segmentation has been the development of international resorts that are designed very specifically for a particular clientele, whether singles, couples, or families. Each of these target markets will respond to different marketing approaches and strategies. Understanding the target market for your particular tourism product or service is a critical starting point for the development of any marketing campaign.

> ➤ In analyzing your market, you need to consider:

  ◆ The total market in size (dollars and units) and growth rate; and

  ◆ Market segments in size (dollars and units) and growth rates.

> ➤ Market segments are groups of customers and potential customers who:

- ◆ Have similar needs and desires that are distinct from other segments; and

- ◆ Can be targeted as a group by adopting unique marketing strategies and tactics.

> ➤ Future trends for each segment should be identified, along with customer needs and wants in each segment.

> ➤ You need to understand how or where segment customers purchase your products or services.

> ➤ What is the profit potential of each segment?

> ➤ A useful technique to determine the attractiveness of market segments is to rank each segment on a scale of 1 to 5 (5 being the best case, 1 being the worst) for the following:

- ◆ Segment size and importance

- ◆ Competition within the segment

- ◆ Fit with your firm's capabilities

- ◆ Growth and profitability potential

- ◆ Market barriers to entry

By totaling up the "score", you get an indication of the attractiveness of each identified segment.

B. COMPETITOR EVALUATION

The tourism industry is more collaborative than many other industries. Different organizations – sometimes direct competitors – have often come together to work towards a common goal, whether that be same-sector associations lobbying government for regulatory change within their industry, or a variety of businesses coming together to market their location as an attractive tourism destination. A recent Canadian Tourism Commission report states, "… the Canadian tourism industry's success depends on how well its stakeholders merge into a strong partnership – one that can understand the market and adapt to change."[2]

Nonetheless, any tourist only has a fixed number of dollars to spend. The large number of choices available to him or her means that they do not need to spend a lot of time or energy trying to find what they are seeking, whether a hotel to stay in, or a restaurant to dine in. Understanding one's competitors, and how your own products compare to theirs, is therefore an important advantage in trying to convince customers to choose your company over one of your competitors.

When analyzing competitors from a marketing perspective, you need to consider the following issues:

➤ What is the market share of your competitors? Have there been any market share changes over the past few years? Why did the changes occur?

➤ Assess your competitors' financial resources, product quality, service and pricing strategies.

➤ Review competing technology attributes (intellectual property protection) and channels of distribution.

➤ Is there potential for competitive actions and reactions to new product or service introductions?

➤ At what stage is the market segment on the product/service life cycle?

C. DISTRIBUTION ANALYSIS

It is important to understand and maximize the effectiveness of your distribution channels. Consider the following:

➤ Where and how does your target market make purchases?

➤ How do you plan to distribute your products and services? How do your competitors distribute their products and services?

➤ Are there other potential distribution channel options? For example, use of the internet has significantly improved distribution opportunities for hotels and other tourism products. What new opportunities may be coming next?

➤ Where is value added in the 'market chain'? Market chain refers to the complete channel from making the product to the ultimate purchase by the final consumer.

➤ How and where does your company add value in the market chain?

➤ How and where do your competitors add value in the market chain? Consider the example of a waterfront hotel that purchases a boat to offer their guests lobster fishing excursions.

➤ Can you partner with appropriate suppliers or distributors to increase value?

D. SUSTAINABLE COMPETITIVE ADVANTAGE REVIEW

The next step is to ask: Do you have a sustainable competitive advantage? You probably do if you meet the following criteria:

> ➤ Competitors find it difficult to imitate your products or services.

> ➤ You have access to a diverse set of markets or market segments.

> ➤ You contribute in a significant way to customers' perceived value of the product or service offered.

Sustainable competitive advantages are generally derived through lower costs, higher quality, added value and specific advantages such as a geographic monopoly, franchise strength or brand image. Further,

> *Among both service and manufacturing industries, the core product sooner or later becomes a commodity as competition increases and the industry matures. As a result, competitive advantage usually emphasizes performance on the supplementary service elements.*[3]

Customer relationship management has become especially important in today's competitive environment, where products and services are more easily replicable. For tourism operators, it's not only what you offer, but how you treat your customers while delivering it, that allow you to stand out above your competitors and give your business the competitive advantage it needs.

E. UNMET CUSTOMER NEEDS ASSESSMENT

In order to identify unmet customers' needs, consider the following:

> ➤ Do you regularly ask your current customers how you could be doing better, or if there are any additional products/services they would like to see you offer?

> ➤ What new needs could be derived from your development of new services, processes, technology, or equipment? For example, in recent years many estate wineries have responded to growing interest in their products and processes by developing regular tasting schedules, and building tasting rooms that will comfortably hold small or large groups.

> ➤ Will new environmental regulations create new opportunities?

> ➤ Do new PEST factors create any further opportunities?

> ➤ Are there any opportunities for increasing value-added products and services?

MARKET RESEARCH

A key component in identifying unmet customer needs is market research. The face of tourism is changing rapidly. Customer interests and needs vary from season to season, and are also strongly influenced by world events. To keep abreast of such changes, or to be the first to introduce an innovative new product to the market, you must have a detailed understanding of your customers and what they are seeking.

Market research is a critical aspect of product development. Tourism operators have a wealth of secondary research (research already undertaken) available to them. More specific, primary research (research you undertake yourself), especially working with one's own existing customers, can also be undertaken. A typical market research process would involve completion of the following steps:

1. Define the marketing issues and the objectives of the research project. What do you want to get out of the project?

2. Develop a research plan. What types of resources are available? What are the expected outcomes? What research approach will be used? How will research participants be identified and contacted?

3. Data collection: it is critical to ensure that the data collected is unbiased to maintain validity. When undertaking surveys or interviews, care must be taken to exclude interviewer bias or questionable answers.

4. Data analysis: once data is collected, a wide variety of statistical and summary techniques can be used to interpret it. These techniques should have been identified in the research plan.

5. Draw conclusions. These will lead to the identification of specific customer wants, needs and will assist in pinpointing target segments. Such conclusions must be logically derived from the research findings.

Secondary research can be undertaken using external sources such as Statistics Canada, the Canadian Tourism Commission, various tourism associations, and Destination Marketing Organizations. Many industry reports and statistics are now available free of charge, on these organizations' corporate websites. Other sector-specific marketing research can be purchased from external research consulting firms. However, you must still do the majority of the analysis yourself in order to draw specific conclusions about your existing or potential products and services.

For tourism operators, research activities might be best focused initially on answering the following important questions regarding the market segment(s) that you are serving:

- ➤ Who are your customers?

- ➤ How many are expected?

- ➤ What interests them?

- ➤ What activities are they looking for?

- ➤ Where do they come from?

- ➤ Why do they travel?

- ➤ Who organizes or hosts their trips?

- ➤ Are they looking for all-inclusive packages?

- ➤ What is their average age?

- ➤ What is their physical condition?

- ➤ What time of year do they travel?

- ➤ How do they travel?

- ➤ How long do they stay in one place?

- ➤ How do they like to spend their money?

- ➤ How much, on average, do they spend per day?

- ➤ What level of service/facilities are they looking for?

- ➤ Are they independent travellers or travelling with a group?[4]

2. MARKETING STRATEGY DEVELOPMENT

Having completed the Market Analysis, we now move on to the development of a specific marketing strategy. This process consists of the following steps:

1. *Vision:* Sets the boundaries of the market-driven activities to be undertaken.

2. *Objectives:* Defines how the vision will be accomplished. These objectives should be SMART (specific, measurable, attainable, relevant and time bound).

3. *Portfolio:* Categorizes the existing portfolio of your products or services. Potential new products and services and their probability for success should also be reviewed.

4. *Segmentation:* Clearly define your target market(s). Which market segments have found your products and services to be the most valuable? Do these segments generate the best financial returns to your firm?

5. *Positioning:* What market tactics (mix of the 4 P's) should be utilized to make your product and services stand out in the minds of your targeted customers? Are there specific ways to differentiate your product offerings?

The "4 P's of Marketing" play a key role in developing a successful tactical strategy. Consider the following use of market tactics:

PRICE

In the tourism industry, decisions about pricing can be influenced by many outside factors. Competitor activities, location, and the time of year can all influence operators to choose different pricing strategies over time.

➢ Your pricing should be set so that it that communicates value to your targeted customers. In pricing your product offerings, complete the following assessment process:

➢ What is the overall pricing objective? Is it to build market share? Maximize revenues? Maximize profits? Achieve product quality leadership?

➢ What are the product costs at different volumes? The higher the accumulated volume, the lower costs can be driven, due to experience curve effects.

➢ How do your prices compare to those of your competitors?

By answering these questions, tourism operators must choose pricing strategies that still meet their organizational needs. Basic costs and expenses must be covered, but profit margins may fluctuate over the course of the year, for example.

PRODUCT

For tourism operators whose product is essentially a service, special attention must be paid to the unique components of the service marketing system, recognizing the importance of all channels through which a customer can learn about, or encounter, your organization. In addition to your customer's experience with the service itself, as provided by front-line personnel hired specifically for this purpose, an overall opinion of the organization is also influenced by all other points of "contact". These include clients' perceptions of the organization's facilities, equipment, and vehicles; communications with other personnel within the organization, such as accounting or housekeeping staff; non-verbal communications from the company, such as signage, invoices, and printed marketing materials; and information provided from other sources, such as word of mouth feedback from other clients, or features in news stories, editorials, or other media sources. Every one of these points of contact provides an opportunity to cultivate a favourable impression within the minds of potential clients. Any inconsistencies can weaken your company's image and credibility.

- ➤ Design and develop products and services so that the targeted customers can easily identify and determine the value that is being delivered to them.

- ➤ Attempt to generate at least one new product development ahead of the marketplace.

- ➤ Be selective when timing the introduction of new products.

PLACE (DISTRIBUTION)

As previously mentioned tourism product distribution channels have undergone much change in recent years. The advent of the Internet and the launch of Global Distribution Systems have changed the way many tourism operators sell their products and services. In addition to traditional distribution channels such as direct selling and using retail travel agents, tourism operators must now also contemplate how best to approach distribution to a global market. In developing your distribution strategy, consider the following:

- ➤ Distribution channel decisions can be complex and challenging, since different channels have different sales methodologies and costs. It is difficult to change channels once established without incurring significant costs and potential loss of sales.

> ➤ Build distribution channels that are consistent with the expectations of your target customers.

> ➤ Channels should be looked upon as partners in your business, working together for mutual benefit.

PROMOTION

For tourism products, advertising and promotion efforts need to be particularly alluring, because travel and tourism products are not "essential" day to day purchases; a customer has to be enticed and encouraged to make the decision to purchase a tourism product.

> ➤ Promotion includes advertising, direct marketing, e-marketing, sales promotions, and public relations for both your firm and product offerings.

> ➤ The key to effective promotion is market and brand awareness.

> ➤ Advertise and promote your product and services in places that your target audiences frequent, and in a manner consistent with the feeling and perceptions that your products and services have created. For example, a country inn promoting their romantic atmosphere may find excellent access to their target client base by having a tradeshow booth at bridal fairs.

For tourism operators, marketing activities to build brand awareness of their local communities can be equally important:

Part of the host [community]'s responsibility is to promote and market their destination. If a host community is to stay competitive it must learn how to market its product effectively. Communities will use destination marketing organizations (DMO) and must be willing to invest the required dollars so that effective promotions for their region and product may be created.

The federal government in the late 1980s learned this lesson the hard way. Canada as a destination was performing well in the mid-1980s, and it rested comfortably in the WTO's list of top 10 tourist destinations. Confident that Canadian tourism was in good shape, the government greatly reduced the tourism marketing budget during the late 1980s. By the early 1990s, Canada's place as a world tourism destination dropped to 14th place.

The Buchanan Report clearly identified this problem and stated that funds needed to be allocated to support a strong marketing program. From a low of $20 million, the federal government and the tourism industry now spend nearly $100 million on a marketing program, sharing the cost on a 50/50 basis. It has paid off. In 1998, the WTO reported that Canada had regained its position in the top 10 tourist destinations, [and ranked in 7th place by 2001].[5]

THREE ADDITIONAL "P's" FOR THE TOURISM INDUSTRY

Recent research[6] has suggested that marketing for the tourism industry requires focus on three additional areas: programming, people, and partnership.

Programming refers to special events or programs that are undertaken specifically to increase consumer awareness and spending on a particular destination, service, or travel package.

People emphasizes that tourism is a people business, that services are ultimately products that are delivered via face to face interactions. Consideration of the human side of customer needs is equally important in marketing efforts as focusing on the product itself.

Partnership reiterates the reality that the tourism industry is made up of many suppliers from many different market segments. Synergies can be created when many operators work together towards common goals.

Note: *Tactics never come before strategy.* Tactics can only be successfully initiated once the marketing strategy development has taken place. Putting tactics before strategy invariably leads to difficulties. For example, creating the product and setting the price before determining customer needs and selecting a target segment, just does not work.

3. MARKET STRATEGY EXECUTION

Once the market strategy development process has been completed, the agreed-upon initiatives and tactics must now be executed. A good execution or implementation plan requires the following:

Communication of the Vision

It is important to ensure that company personnel buy into your company's marketing vision and its products and services.

Development of Skills and Competencies

You need to assess what skills your people need to execute the vision. Do they have them now? Can they be developed? Can you acquire them?

Establishing Incentives

Proper incentives are required to motivate your people to perform the required market- driven tasks and initiatives. Lack of proper incentives will lead to slower execution and change. Incentives can be either financial or non-financial.

Acquiring Resources

The execution of a market strategy cannot be successfully accomplished without having the necessary resources to implement the plan. A lack of required resources (such as the appropriate people, financing, strategic partners) causes frustration and lack of motivation.

Development of the Appropriate Organizational Structure

An appropriate market-oriented structure needs to be set up with clearly defined lines of authority and responsibility in place. The structure should be linked to key success factors that have been developed by involving all key persons in your company. There will then be more motivation to achieve specific accomplishment targets that have been mutually agreed upon.

Detail the Execution Plan

The market strategy execution plan needs to be detailed in writing, indicating responsibilities, performance benchmarks and timelines. "The marketing plan for a destination or a firm is one of the most important working documents that exists. It serves to translate the many ideals of tourism policy into an active process for attracting visitors and providing the range of experiences they seek from a destination."[7]

USEFUL WEB SITES:

www.marketingsherpa.com	Case studies in sales and marketing for companies selling into internet markets
www.strategymag.com	Canadian marketing report with a focus on information-based marketing
www.the-cma.org	Canadian Marketing Association
http://research.canadatourism.com/en/ctc/ctc_index.cfm	Canadian Tourism Exchange
www.tiac-aitc.ca	Tourism Industry Association of Canada (TIAC)
www.ttra.com	Travel and Tourism Research Association
www.hotelassociation.ca	Hotel Association of Canada (HAC)
www.crfa.ca	Canadian Restaurant and Foodservices Association
www.foodserviceworld.com/hotelier	Hotelier Magazine
www.hotel-online.com	Hotel Online

Endnotes

1. Lovelock, Christopher H., *Managing Services: Marketing, Operations and Human Resources, 2nd Edition.* Prentice Hall, New Jersey, 1992, pp. 19.

2. The American Tourism Market: *Evolution to 2010: It's Coming Faster Than You Think.* Canadian Tourism Commission, 2003.

3. Lovelock, pp. 27.

4. *Starting A Tourism Business.* Tourism British Columbia, 2003, pp. 35

5. Polovitz, Norma, *Snapshots: an introduction to tourism, 3rd Canadian Edition,* Pearson / Prentice Hall, Toronto, 2004, pp. 56.

6. Mill, R. C., and A.M. Morrison. *The Tourism System: An Introductory Text, 4th edition.* Kendall/Hunt, Dubuque, 2002.

7. Goeldner, Charles R., and Ritchie, J.R. Brent. *Tourism Principles Practices Philosophies, 9th Edition.* John Wiley & Sons, New Jersey, 2003, pp. 548

CHAPTER 5
THE OPERATIONS REVIEW

OVERVIEW

The manner in which a business conducts its basic operations is an important element in the Size-Up process. In this section, the following key areas will be covered:

- Business Operations
- Risk Management Issues
- Legal Concerns
- Location Decisions
- Technology Considerations

BUSINESS OPERATIONS

THE OPERATIONS PROCESS

In their simplest form, operations consist of the completion of activities that are necessary to get the task performed. The operations process transforms inputs into outputs. The end result is the successful delivery of a product or service that meets customers' quality requirements and expectations.

A key outcome of this function is the improved productivity of the company which allows it to compete more effectively in its marketplace. Generally, organizations with higher productivity possess a superior competitive advantage.

Operations are not an isolated function. They are closely intertwined with the other functional areas of the business – especially finance, marketing and human resources. At times, conflict can arise between these different functional areas. Tourism operators can gain a bird's eye perspective on competing priorities by understanding the four key pressure points for any business:

- ➢ What do we, the managers of this business, want? (Finance department)
- ➢ What do our customers want? (Marketing department)
- ➢ What do our staff and suppliers want? (Human Resources department)
- ➢ What are we capable of doing? (Operations department)

Where these four priorities intersect/overlap is where managers should focus their attention, and design their operations processes to maximize as much benefit as possible.

PRODUCTS VERSUS SERVICES

IMPLICATIONS:

- ➢ Service firms have greater direct customer contact. Individuals providing services normally have more face-to-face contact with customers than those individuals performing manufacturing operations.

- ➢ For tourism operators offering services to their customers, the importance of job design is critical. A key consideration for any business' success and profitability is ensuring that clients receive the best possible experience without demanding "impossible" levels of performance from employees, or overtaxing the facilities and equipment that are required for service delivery.

- ➢ For the human side of this job design equation, the importance of recruitment, training, authority, and career management are discussed in more detail in the following chapter.

- ➢ Product manufacturing operations can build or deplete product inventories to meet demand cycles, whereas service providers cannot "store up" their services. They have to adopt strategies that level out the demand process. "Capacity planning is vital in capacity-constrained service organizations which need to match productive resources to fluctuating demand levels."[1]

> ➤ Tourism operators need to strategize on how to manage this reality, and its effects on service quality. For example, seasonal employment results in higher training costs, whereas year-round employment may result in waste and employee boredom during times of low demand. All pros and cons need to be examined and measured.

> ➤ Quality standards are more difficult to establish and measure in service operations. Service standardization has been employed by some tourism operators, such as franchised restaurants. This strict attention to detailed processes and procedures often results in lower costs and consistent quality. However, it may also encourage employee boredom and lack of flexibility in problem solving, which can have their own effects on customers.

> ➤ Quality control in service industries is difficult for exactly this reason: quality is only ever defined by customer perceptions of services received. This can present a moving target to tourism operators seeking a clear definition of what "quality" means in their own companies, and how they can measure it. Regular monitoring of customer satisfaction is therefore especially important. It is encouraging to note that in spite of the extra effort required to effectively introduce quality control measures in service business, nonetheless in recent years a number of international hotels have been successful in achieving ISO 9000[2] certification.

> ➤ Productivity is generally easier to measure in production operations. Improving productivity for service providers means that the value or volume of outputs (services provided) improves in relation to the value or volume of inputs required for service delivery.

> ➤ Regardless of the methods chosen by managers to achieve this goal – which can range from working employees harder, to avoiding bottlenecks in the service delivery process – the gains are again highly dependent upon customers' perceptions of the results. Analysis needs to be undertaken, to determine whether cost savings in one area might have a resultant negative effect upon the value of the service being purchased by the client.

GUIDELINES FOR ASSESSING BUSINESS OPERATIONS

PROCESS EMPLOYED

What type of production/service delivery process is employed?

> ♦ Tourism operators can greatly benefit from undertaking a service blueprint analysis of their operations. "The intangibility surrounding a service complicates the traditional management tasks of planning, organizing, directing and controlling the performances which go into

creating a service. If a way can be found to depict the service system concretely, the service management task is not only simplified but important elements of control are gained as well."[3]

◆ A service blueprint is customer-focused, looking at processes from the perspective of a client's experience with the company, along the service delivery path. It shows what happens in all processes, by whom, to whom, when, and how. Every customer contact with the organization is identified; managers can be surprised to see how many individual contacts form a customer's overall impression of their company.

For example, a customer's experience in a hotel is formed by many points of contact, from viewing initial marketing materials (physical brochures or on the internet), to telephone conversations with reservations staff, to the check-in experience, to being greeted by housekeeping staff, to being served dinner in the restaurant, to understanding the documentation of the final bill at check out.. Each of these individual points of contact form the customer's overall impression of their experience, and a negative experience in any single interaction can undo all other positive experiences.

◆ By documenting the service delivery process with this attention to detail, managers can identify aspects of delivery systems that may otherwise have been hidden or overlooked, and be able to analyze the entire service experience as a whole, so as to identify new efficiencies and economies.

➢ How does the production process relate to the firm's marketing strategies?

◆ Sales and marketing activities need to recognize all processes used in service delivery. The power of a dissatisfied customer and their potential to generate a negative impact on your business is very high. It is estimated that satisfied customers may tell five of their acquaintances about their experience, whereas a dissatisfied customer will tell twenty.

◆ Word of mouth is a vital marketing tool that is gaining even more credibility in our age of marketing message bombardment; a service recovery system must therefore be in place to manage and correct those situations where service delivery has not met customer needs. Related to this, managers must ensure that all promises made by sales personnel and marketing campaigns can be delivered, every time. Capacity realities, and other resource constraints faced by the company, must be kept in mind at all times.

> What types of equipment and technologies are being used? Are any changes required or planned in order to remain competitive?

 ◆ Can outsourcing improve the bottom line by allowing employees to focus their attentions on other areas? Is the equipment being used for service delivery current? Managers working in a service environment need to pay as much attention to equipment and technology as manufacturers do.

 ◆ Although services are delivered through human interaction, service providers nonetheless still need the best tools available to excel in their jobs.

FACILITIES MANAGEMENT

Facilities management is an important aspect of operations for any tourism business that welcomes customers onto their premises. Every detail of the guest's experience should be anticipated in advance. It is easy to focus attention solely on the actual product or service that the guest is there to purchase (for example, does the hotel guest get a room to sleep in?)

However, even if the basics are covered, the overall experience of the guest is also greatly impacted by how the product or service is delivered. Cleanliness and high levels of service are part of the product, and more and more are the means by which tourism companies differentiate themselves from one another. Facilities management includes the following:

> shift scheduling to ensure all areas of service delivery are adequately covered.

> housekeeping procedures and staffing to ensure cleanliness standards are met.

> engineering and maintenance planning, so that there is no down time or guest disruptions due to mechanical failures or utilities problems.

> hiring grounds keeping and interior design staff when required to maintain a welcoming environment for guests.

> effective management of outsourced services for the company.

> planning for maintenance and renovations well in advance in order to minimize disruptions to guests.

CAPACITY

1. What is the capacity of the facility and how close is current output to that capacity?

Yield management is particularly important in many tourism businesses. When capacity is fixed, choosing the most profitable reservations/guests can make a significant difference to a company's bottom line. Analysis of guest demographics and spending patterns should reveal which market segment is the most profitable.

Efforts can then be focused to attract and retain this specific group of customers, and to ensure that every effort is made to offer these guests as many spending high-yield purchase opportunities as possible.

2. Are there any plans to increase capacity? What are the associated costs?

For tourism companies, it is often very expensive to increase capacity. Airlines need to purchase additional aircraft; hotels need to build more rooms; restaurants need to expand their premises. For this reason, service providers should first concentrate their efforts for improved profitability on marketing and yield management techniques to fill current capacity before considering expansion.

The time to consider adding capacity is when customer demand consistently outstrips a company's ability to accommodate everyone.

3. Is production/service delivery planning a difficult task? Is demand difficult to estimate?

Many tourism operators book their customers in advance. Tracking trends by examining the company's sales data against seasons, marketing efforts, and even local events such as fairs and festivals, can assist managers to better predict demand and plan service delivery accordingly.

4. What are the near term capital expenditure (capex) requirements?

Managers must never lose sight of the bottom line. If equipment needs updating, or an expansion is warranted, plans need to be made well in advance in order to access the necessary funding.

INVENTORY

1. What type of inventory is carried (raw materials, work in process, finished goods)?

The inventory in tourism businesses is mostly perishable and often intangible. Inventory is always "carried", whether that is a seat on a tour bus, a table at a restaurant, or a room in a hotel. Nonetheless, even for tourism operators who sell services, there are specific tangible inputs/supplies required in order to achieve service delivery. Restaurants need food and drink supplies. Airlines need fuel. Hotels need cleaning supplies and linens. Inventory management is essential to successful service delivery.

2. How are inventories managed?

Effective documentation, tracking, and analysis are required to avoid shortages of critical supplies. Decisions must be made regarding how much of each item to stock, versus how much to rely on just-in-time delivery from suppliers. Further, if your company only has a single supplier for an inventory item that is essential to your service delivery, acknowledge this as vulnerability and take the time to source a backup supplier.

3. Consider the following inventory management objectives:

 ♦ Minimize inventory investment by carrying smaller inventories which result in lower financing, storage, and obsolescence costs.

 ♦ Keep work in process on schedule.

 ♦ Maximizing sales and product selection (keeping sufficient inventory to avoid stock outs and missed sales opportunities).

 ♦ Guarding against deterioration, shrinkage or theft.

WORK FORCE

1. Who manages the operations? What is their background and capability?

Tourism businesses often promote staff from within into management or supervisory roles. It is essential that new managers and supervisors are given the appropriate tools and training to be effective in their new roles. If a staff member is going to be responsible for managing a kitchen or a laundry facility, they need to understand inventory management. The company should invest in the necessary training to ensure the success of their people in their new roles.

2. What is the nature of the work force (numbers, key skills, local labor supply)?

Tourism operators face special challenges in the area of human resources management. This is discussed in detail in the following chapter.

3. What are the company's practices regarding full-time versus part-time workers, layoffs, compensation, and union/management relations?

Managing these issues is particularly important for tourism operators whose businesses are seasonal in nature.

QUALITY

"Quality is the degree of excellence intended, and the control of variability in achieving that excellence, in meeting the customer's requirements."[4]

1. How important is production/service delivery quality?

For tourism operators, the importance of service delivery quality cannot be overstated. The service is the product, and the customer's perception of its quality is entirely subjective. Quality management is essential. Because service delivery involves the actual participation of the customer, risks are higher than for companies manufacturing tangible products. Restaurants cannot serve contaminated food. Airlines cannot fly faulty aircraft. Hotels cannot house guests in a facility with no fire alarms or sprinkler systems. When the risks to customers' physical persons are this high, service delivery quality must be given the highest priority.

2. How is quality controlled? Are there Quality Management (QM) programs in place?

ISO 9000 was mentioned above; attaining such certification is a well recognized signal of quality excellence. However, the process of ISO 9000 certification is expensive and complicated. This should not deter smaller firms from pursuing their own Quality Management programs, however. Four essential points need to be considered:

♦ A thorough and ongoing understanding of customer requirements is the starting point of quality management. "Quality" exists only where customer needs are being met.

♦ A company's entire operations must focus on quality. A lapse of attention to quality at any point in service delivery operations will compromise the total effort. Managers, staff, and even suppliers must all adhere to a quality focus in every aspect of service delivery.

♦ Over time, it costs a firm more to respond to lapses in quality, or service delivery failures, than it does to invest in a quality management system in the first place.

♦ Inspection and performance reviews by managers must not simply identify and acknowledge service failures, but instead must concentrate effort on fixing the inherent causes of service failure, in order to avoid subsequent incidents.

3. Are there any product return policies or customer complaint implications?

Tourism companies dedicated to quality management must give their customers the opportunity to complain. Such feedback is priceless in terms of giving managers the opportunity to fix problems in the service delivery process.

Make it easy for customers to give their feedback (guest comment cards, a final inquiry upon departure), respond professionally and promptly, and thank the customer for giving you their valuable feedback.

RISK MANAGEMENT ISSUES

Comprehensive Program

Risk management (managing risk factors) involves the implementation of programs that preserve assets and the earning power of the business. Whereas quality management programs are implemented in an effort to prevent problems, risk management programs must be put in place to also deal with problems if and when they do occur.

As mentioned above, due to the inherent nature of personal contact with customers when tourism companies provide services to their clients, having a comprehensive risk management program is very important. For tourism operators especially, risk management has taken on a much more important role than in the past, with the terrible incidents of terrorism and natural disasters that have recently impacted the industry so deeply.

Hazards

In the development of a risk management program, any potential hazards for customers or employees must first be identified, along with a detailed account of the means by which the potentially dangerous product or process is encountered. Heating systems, boiler rooms, elevators, and kitchens all have the potential for accidents and injuries to occur.

Regular maintenance and upgrades, and adherence to industry best practices in working with hazardous machinery and products, are required. Security systems must also be given attention; from automated room locks to nightclub bouncers, every hospitality firm needs a solid plan in place to manage the systems that protect its guests.

Tracking

Once areas of risk and system procedures have been identified, a tracking program should be implemented, to document any incidents or accidents that have occurred to date. Based on this data, a comprehensive staff training program is the next important step. Staff must be trained in detail, not only on how to prevent accidents, but also on how to react when an incident occurs.

Staff must also understand the impact that previous incidents have had on the company, both monetarily and in terms of public perception.

External Factors

In addition to risk management for on-site situations, manager must also address emergency planning for situations such as natural or other disasters. In cases of fire, flood, earthquake, illness, or security breaches, managers must plan in advance how they will handle such situations. An emergency plan must be developed, with input and validation from all staff. Ask the question "what if?" and follow through to cover all possible situations and their impacts.

Drills should be conducted to practice planned responses. Emergency supplies must be accessible: food, water, flashlights, power generators, mobile phones, first aid supplies, propane tanks, baby supplies, extension cords, and battery-powered radios.

A communications plan should also be developed which anticipates what messages will need to be sent, to whom, by whom, and when. Ideally at least one staff member will be trained in media relations to skillfully guide the company through communications on any emergency situations. Certainly the forest fires in British Columbia during the summer of 2003 highlighted the need for all such preparations.

Benefits

Having a comprehensive risk management program in place benefits tourism operators to lower costs by planning in advance to meet risk management targets both in incident prevention and in effective incident handling. It also demonstrates to a company's insurance providers that they are serious about managing the care and safety of employees and customers.

Finally, where a solid risk management plan is in place, a company can even leverage this by making their customers aware of their efforts, in marketing materials and other communications. Now, more than ever, customers are asking questions about their safety before purchasing any product or service.

INSURANCE

Tourism businesses that provide services to their customers are often at higher risk for liability issues. Just as doctors and other service providers have faced skyrocketing insurance costs, so too has the tourism industry recently seen significant increases in their premiums. A 2003 report by the Council of Tourism Associations of British Columbia on Insurance and Financing states:

In property insurance ... for midsize and small property accounts increases in the 10 to 20 percent range may occur. On liability insurance there could be rate increases of between 20 and 50 percent on general liability.[5]

Thus, more than ever, it is a worthwhile investment of time to examine your insurance needs carefully and compare the variety of products available to you. Insurance protection is an integral part of a sound risk management program.

MAJOR TYPES OF BUSINESS INSURANCE

> Commercial Property Insurance: Covers damages resulting from fire, storm, theft and other dangers. Many policies cover 'all risks' (any damage that is not specifically excluded).

> General Liability Insurance: Is usually combined with property coverage in a standard business owners' policy and covers legal defense costs if someone is injured on your property or by your product. Food and Liquor Liability, Non-owned Automobile Liability, Third Party Property Damage, and Innkeepers Liability all fall under the category of general liability insurance and should be carefully assessed.

> Auto Insurance: Comprehensive insurance, collision, liability, accident benefits, loss of use.

> Business Interruption Insurance: Covers fixed expenses that would continue if, for example, a fire shuts down the business.

> Key Person Insurance: Covers the loss of key people in your business through death or prolonged disability that can result in reduced profitability.

> Buy-Sell Insurance: A life insurance policy for each company owner's share of the business. If one of the owners dies, a cash settlement is received by his/her estate/family in exchange for his/her business interests.

> Business Loan Insurance: Offered through lenders, who receive insurance proceeds to retire company loan principal after the death of the business owner.

> Group Insurance: Tailored to provide a combination of life, health, dental, and disability insurance for the benefit of business employees and their families.

> Credit Insurance: Protects businesses from unexpected bad debts.

> Surety Bonds: Insure against failure of other firms to complete contractual obligations. Frequently used in the construction industry.

> Fidelity Insurance Bonds: Protect businesses against losses incurred from theft or other financial loss caused by their employees.

LEGAL ISSUES

OWNERSHIP STRUCTURE

There are four basic paths to owning your own business:

> ➤ You can start your own new business from scratch. Under this scenario, particular attention should be paid to whether there is market share available for your new business in the marketplace for your product/service.
>
> Unless your chosen business is in a growth market or your business is sufficiently unique to attract a new market, your survival will otherwise depend on taking market share away from existing companies in the sector.

> ➤ You can purchase a franchise. The security provided by buying into a proven formula can be attractive to some business owners. Franchises still allow the owner independence and profit sharing, while minimizing some of the sector risk.

> ➤ You can purchase an existing business as a "going concern". Caveat empor is important under this scenario, as the purchaser must assure himself or herself that the business has an established customer base and reputation. However, financing may be easier to secure under this option.

> ➤ You can buy the assets of an existing business that is declaring bankruptcy. This may be the least attractive option, because it is often difficult to shake a bad reputation from the former management. However, the chance to purchase property or equipment at great savings may outweigh this risk.

Once you have decided on which route you will take to business ownership, you must then decide which legal structure you should adopt. Here are three basic options:

1. Sole proprietorship

2. Partnership

3. Corporation

1. SOLE PROPRIETORSHIP

Key features:

➤ You own the business outright and your business income is treated as personal income. This is the simplest form of business ownership. Sole proprietorship companies must pay taxes on the business income and have a license to operate. Company names (other than the owner's own name) must be officially registered.

Advantages:

➤ Business losses can be offset against your personal taxable income.

➤ Lower costs of set-up and operation.

➤ Less regulation and reporting requirements.

➤ All profits go to the owner of the company.

Disadvantages:

➤ Limited access to capital.

➤ You are personally liable for all business obligations and any related litigation.

➤ Some government programs are only available to incorporated entities.

➤ High dependence on owner's presence in maintaining operational continuity.

2. PARTNERSHIPS

Key features:

➤ Each partner shares in profits/losses based on their percentage interest in the business.

➤ The partners' responsibilities and obligations are normally defined in a written partnership agreement.

Advantages:

- ➤ Workload and capital requirements are shared.

- ➤ New partners can be added, thereby providing more flexibility.

- ➤ Partners provide different skill sets, mutual support, and more potential sources of capital.

- ➤ Partners are taxed individually.

- ➤ There are few legal restrictions, and therefore lower expenses.

Disadvantages:

- ➤ Unlimited liability for partnership debts.

- ➤ Business and personal assets are at risk for any financial losses suffered.

- ➤ One partner can potentially make decisions that bind all others.

- ➤ Dissolution can be difficult and time consuming.

Note: There are limited liability partnerships (LLPs) that limit the amount of personal liability. These are generally used in professional service organizations.

3. CORPORATIONS

Key features:

- ➤ A separate legal entity granted authority by either federal or provincial law.

- ➤ Legally separate from the owners (shareholders).

Advantages:

- ➤ Greater access to sources of capital via share issues (equity) and security agreements (debt).

- ➤ Expanded estate planning benefits.

- ➤ Shareholders are not personally responsible for corporations' debts (unless personal guarantees have been signed).

➤ Enhanced image via corporate profile.

➤ Internal incentives available to employees (i.e. stock options).

➤ Business is not dependent on specific individuals for company continuity.

Disadvantages:

➤ Higher start-up costs and a more complex regulatory environment.

➤ Potentially fewer tax write-offs at commencement of business operations.

➤ Corporations must disclose many details about their operations and therefore there is less privacy.

Engaging an experienced and skilled commercial lawyer is an essential element to the operations planning process especially before any significant business commitments or decisions are made. Your commercial lawyer can assist in the following areas:

➤ Business incorporation and partnership agreement structuring.

➤ Setting up and negotiating commercial property leases.

➤ Protecting intellectual property.

➤ Reviewing franchise agreements.

➤ Resolving employment issues (terminations, severance agreements).

➤ Initiating overdue receivable collections.

➤ Drafting buy/sell agreements between shareholders.

➤ Structuring legal contracts (joint ventures co-ownership agreements, licensing agreements, etc.).

➤ Acquisition agreements (buying/selling assets or shares) along with the necessary due diligence.

LEGAL ENVIRONMENT

In addition to the legal details involved in setting up a business, tourism operators must also be aware of legal issues at a broader level. Changes in the regulatory environment can have a significant impact on certain businesses, and it's important to stay on top of such changes at both the local and federal levels. The following areas of tourism operations have experienced change in recent years, and/or seen an increase in litigation activity:

> ➤ Anti-smoking laws

> ➤ Food safety, including allergy awareness and nutrition issues

> ➤ Alcohol sales and service

> ➤ Property maintenance

> ➤ Hotel and airline overbooking

> ➤ Property theft

> ➤ Vandalism

> ➤ Room security

> ➤ Travel security

> ➤ SOCAN music licensing

> ➤ Employment standards

> ➤ Harassment and discrimination

> ➤ Environmental protection and sustainability regulation

It is the responsibility of business owners to be well informed of all legal issues affecting their operations, and to do everything within their power to protect their employees, customers, and visitors. Participation in industry associations, and/or subscription to trade journals are excellent ways of staying informed about such issues, and every business owner should have ready access to legal counsel and representation.

LOCATION OF PHYSICAL FACILITIES

The location decision for a company owner is an important one and can range from operating a home office to purchasing, leasing or renting a commercial building.

There are five key factors in determining an appropriate location:

1) Financial

- ♦ Cost of land and improvements.

- ♦ Current property leases.

- ♦ Local labour costs and tax structures.

2) Personal Preferences

- ◆ Proximity to home.

- ◆ Colleagues, friends, or relatives close by.

3) Market Access

- ◆ Convenience for clients and suppliers.

- ◆ Proximity to target markets.

4) Resource availability

- ◆ Accessibility to raw materials.

- ◆ Effective transportation links and communications.

- ◆ Qualified labor force and management.

5) Environmental Conditions

- ◆ Local laws and regulatory structure. Government support and incentives.

- ◆ Climate.

- ◆ Quality of life.

HOME OFFICES

Many small companies commence operations as home-based businesses. This decision is usually driven by cost considerations and the fact that business is in an early growth stage. There are obvious advantages with a home-based business scenario but such arrangements may not work for everyone. Potential downsides include:

- ➤ Client demands and expectations. Working from home can lead to longer response times, especially if colleagues are in separate locations.

- ➤ Adverse zoning by-laws.

- ➤ Lack of focus. Too many distractions from family and neighborhood.

- ➤ Difficulty in maintaining spatial boundaries between business and home.

INCUBATORS

Business incubators provide early-stage entrepreneurs with affordable space, clerical assistance, and, sometimes, mentorship facilities. Many are funded by government agencies and/or universities and appear to be a growing trend. Benefits include:

- ➤ Access to legal and /accounting services.
- ➤ Profile and credibility.
- ➤ Access to investing 'angels' and venture capital sources.

LEASE OR BUY

Early stage companies invariably lease premises and often commence operations by renting space on a short-term (month-to-month) basis before entering into longer term and more formalized lease arrangements.

- ➤ Advantages to leasing (for both established companies or start-ups):
  - ◆ Preservation of capital for other uses. While this is somewhat obvious for start-ups, many established companies fail to recognize the significant impact that a property purchase decision will have on their working capital and future potential.

  Example: Company XYZ purchases a commercial property for $1 million and obtains $600,000 in long-term financing (with loan payments equivalent to lease payments) and the balance of the purchase funded by $400,000 in cash. The $400,000 cash outflow *reduces* the company's working capital resources. (These funds could have been used to identify additional markets and then launch a new generation of product lines providing enhanced revenue and earnings performance).

  - ◆ Greater flexibility: Ability to relocate at the end of the lease term and find larger premises, if necessary.
  - ◆ Fluctuations in local property values (especially decreases in market values) do not affect the value of the company.
- ➤ Advantages of buying
  - ◆ Able to modify or customize property.
  - ◆ No third party relationship to landlord.
  - ◆ May enjoy property value appreciation.
  - ◆ Surplus space could be leased out.

TECHNOLOGY CONSIDERATIONS

The impact of technology on tourism operations is a huge and rapidly evolving topic. In this section we provide a brief summary of computer technology applications which impact company operations and an overview of e-commerce opportunities and strategies.

COMPUTER TECHNOLOGY APPLICATIONS

Computer technology is widely used to track financial and marketing activities and transactions.

- Local Area Networks (LAN) have dramatically improved office automation.

- Customized software is now extensively used for tasks such as reservations, payroll, inventory management, billing and accounting.

- Productivity software (word processing, spreadsheets, database management) has generated significant cost savings.

- Significant improvements in office communications technology have taken place through e-mail, voicemail, cell phones, pagers, Personal Digital Assistants (PDAs), and video conferencing systems.

- Business presentations have been enhanced via multimedia technology that integrates text, audio, graphics, and video.

E-COMMERCE OPPORTUNITIES

Some of the opportunities and issues arising from the rapidly growing world of e-commerce include:

A. Business to Consumer Transactions (B2C)

- Emarketer, Inc. forecasts annual US consumer spending via B2C transactions to top US$109 billion in 2004[6]. Despite the recent dot.com upheaval, growth in this market has continued steadily, partially in response to increased use of broadband Internet access around the world.

- Credit card transactions are a key element of the B2C world. Appropriate security and technology standards are crucial and, while generally secure, are continually being refined.

B. Business to Business Transactions (B2B)

Recent research estimates U.S. B2B revenues for 2003 to top $634 billion[7]. These expenditures have grown dramatically over recent years, easily surpassing the historical growth rates observed in the B2C sector. Why? The reason is simple. There are far more separate transactions involving buyers and sellers in the business world. There are two types of B2B companies:

1. Vertical companies: These firms create markets within certain industries (e.g., steel, life sciences, chemicals), thereby allowing companies within the given industry (vertical) to electronically communicate and transact with potential suppliers and customers.

2. Horizontal companies: These companies serve the same needs across different industries. For example:

   ♦ Raw goods procurement – Commerce One and Ariba

   ♦ Finished goods shipment -Fedex and UPS

Benefits derived from engaging in B2B e-commerce include:

➢ Reduced purchasing costs.

➢ Increased market efficiency with price quotes quickly available from numerous suppliers.

➢ Increased market intelligence which provides greater understanding of demand levels in any given market.

➢ Decreased inventory levels that arise from enhanced 'just in time' processes.

➢ Increased capacity utilization with excess inventory being turned over via selective online auctions.

USEFUL WEB SITES:

www.ibcpub.com	Logistics Business magazine
www.onvia.com	Operations guidelines for small business
http://laws.justice.gc.ca	Canada Department of Justice
www.iso.org/iso/en/iso9000-14000/index.html	ISO 9000 description and information

Endnotes

1. Lovelock, Christopher H., *Managing Services: Marketing, Operations and Human Resources, 2nd Edition*. Prentice Hall, New Jersey, 1992, pp. 400.

2. ISO 9000 is a certification granted by the International Standards Organization to companies that meet strict criteria in their operations to consistently achieve superior results.

3. Lovelock, pg. 96.

4. Lovelock, pg. 239.

5. British Columbia Tourism Industry *Insurance and Financing Report*, December 2003. http://www.cotabc.com/documents/Temporary/Insurance%20%20Financing%20Report%20-%20Executive%20Summary.pdf

6. US B2C E-Commerce Tops $90B This Year, April 29, 2003. http://www.gcis.ca/n-aa/cdne-500-may-01-2003.html

7. *Business Market: The Growth of B2B Market, 2003.* http://ecommerce.insightin.com/market_research/business_market.html

CHAPTER 6
HUMAN RESOURCES MANAGEMENT

OVERVIEW

In this section, we review the human resources function and examine key characteristics of leadership. Many smaller, early stage companies tend to minimize the importance of this functional area.

Human resources management is a key contributor to an organization's health and has a strong influence on a company's competitive position in the marketplace. Particularly in the tourism sector, finding great people to represent your firm, and retaining them as satisfied, long-term employees, is becoming more difficult as the available labour pool continues to shrink.

The industry is faced with other issues as well: negative perceptions about the quality of tourism jobs, too little focus on retention strategies, and a gap in the availability of training and education programs that are needed by the industry.

As demand for tourism products continues to grow – especially now in light of Vancouver's successful bid to host the Winter Olympics in 2010 – adopting effective human resources management practices is an important way in which tourism operators can prepare themselves for growth and success.

1. THE HUMAN RESOURCE (HR) FUNCTION

Key areas:

> ➤ Recruitment and hiring

> ➤ Training and development

> ➤ Compensation and incentives

> ➤ Performance

> ➤ Retention

> ➤ Planning (short and long term)

RECRUITMENT AND HIRING

Hiring and retaining motivated employees, who either support or interface directly with your clients, is a critical success factor. It has never been more important for tourism companies to compete for talent and take steps to retain good staff.

Issues to consider:

> ➤ The critical importance of 'hiring right'. Service managers must resist the temptation to either hire staff that do not have the skills necessary to work effectively with clientele one on one, or worse, to leave positions unfilled in an effort to save money. Any drop in service levels will be quickly detected by customers, and poor service interactions can have disastrous results. Hiring strategies are necessarily time consuming, but pay off in the end. "Managers need to compete as hard and creatively for talent market share as they compete for sales market share... Recommended: Market careers rather than jobs, market them in multiple ways, link hiring standards to service standards, and leverage the freedom factor [autonomy to problem solve]."[1]

> ➤ For service companies, the use of aptitude testing has been shown to be effective in personnel selection, particularly for positions that require a high degree of customer interaction. There is a high correlation between service effectiveness and having particular service-oriented personality characteristics (such as a caring attitude, or helpfulness).

> ➤ The need to demonstrate to new employees their ability to progress to positions of greater responsibility. This has been another industry challenge, identified by recent government and industry studies. Historically, many tourism managers have been placed into their roles by working their way up in their companies from entry-level positions.

♦ They may not value the importance of training for their staff. Employees can become frustrated at the lack of opportunities, and higher turnover results. Several new initiatives, from both government and industry, are working to improve this, through the development of new, accessible education and training programs, occupational standards, and accreditation programs that recognize industry experience.

Sources of new employees:

➤ Employee referrals.

➤ Employment agencies and tourism employment programs.

➤ Newspaper advertisements.

➤ Educational institutions (internships, co-op programs, career fairs).

➤ Competitors.

Selection and evaluation of new employees. Some issues to consider:

➤ Pro-forma job application forms.

➤ A formalized interview process.

➤ References (extensive due diligence is required).

➤ Determine who has the responsibility for hiring. Does this tie in with reporting relationships?

TRAINING AND DEVELOPMENT

Retaining good existing employees is a key strategy which requires the establishment of appropriate performance-based evaluation systems and a culture that promotes workplace quality, pride and achievement. Tourism operators are encouraged to take the extra steps required to ensure that employees are thoroughly trained in their duties, offered new opportunities for learning and training, and receive appropriate recognition when their performance meets or exceeds expectations.

Issues to consider:

➤ Ineffective training programs can lead to trial and error learning, and varying levels of service quality.

➤ Orientation of new employees should include an explanation of specific job duties, performance expectations and evaluation processes. The use of standard job descriptions may help to communicate responsibilities and expectations.

➤ The importance of ongoing quality management (QM) training should be supported by a formalized training plan, timetable and feedback process. Any tourism worker needs to know the importance of offering quality products and services, and the negative impact that results when delivery falls short. Tourism operators who regularly hire front-line employees need to ensure that newcomers fully understand the company's quality standards, and why they are important to profitability.

➤ Developing high performing employees for progression into marketing, sales and management positions involves retraining and the creation of new career paths. In preparation for the 2010 Olympics, thousands of new managers and supervisors will be hired, and many of these positions will be filled by promoting staff from within. Training and education programs are needed for these new positions, not only in the specific skills required by the industry sector, but also in people skills, HR practices, and overall business management.

COMPENSATION AND INCENTIVES

➤ Employee incentives can be both financial and non-financial. Research shows that giving appropriate recognition and thanks when an employee performs well goes a long way towards the promotion of job satisfaction, and helps to alleviate the risks of service staff burnout. Where salary levels are equal, industries that have improved their HR practices consistently attract and retain more employees. Companies should offer a motivating environment with open communication, mutual respect and flexibility for their staff.

➤ Financial compensation must be in line with competitors and should be monitored and reviewed on a regular basis. Salary standards for a wide range of industry positions can be accessed from industry consultants.

➤ Performance-based compensation systems (profit-sharing plans) need to be carefully designed. This is best accomplished by using external HR specialists, although the cost of this service may be a deterrent to smaller companies.

➤ Where industry norms dictate, comprehensive benefits packages may also need to be developed (vacation, medical and dental and life and disability insurance plans).

➤ Employee equity incentive plans: employees often have the opportunity to participate in a company's financial growth by way of various equity incentive plans. These include:

◆ Group RRSP plans

◆ Stock purchase plans

- ◆ Profit sharing
- ◆ Stock options

➤ Stock options provide the right to purchase company common shares at a stated price during a specific period of time. Usually, options are granted with an exercise price equal to the fair market value of the stock at date of grant or hire. If the stock price rises above the exercise price, the option allows the employee to purchase the stock at a lower (exercise) price.

➤ Vesting periods are the periods of time during which the options are held by the employee but cannot be triggered. There is usually a minimum one-year waiting period often followed by 'stepped' vesting periods over the next three to four years.

➤ Liquidity issues: While there is a potential financial gain to the employee (derived when the stock exercise price is less than the current market value), liquidity (the ability to sell the stock) remains a key consideration, especially if private company shares have been vested.

➤ Such incentive programs have the indirect benefit of locking in (or hand-cuffing) key employees, thereby reducing the risk of their departure to competitors. Clear ground rules need to be established as to the stock disposition process when the employee departs (especially if to a competitor).

PERFORMANCE

Goal setting should be established on an annual basis and linked to a formal performance evaluation process (informally every quarter, formally every year). The goal-setting process should include:

➤ Job objectives/responsibilities. Industry standards for a wide variety of tourism jobs are now available and can be helpful in this regard.

➤ Performance criteria to be used in annual review: exceeded/ achieved/ did not achieve plan.

➤ Performance assessment should include both qualitative and quantitative factors. Criteria and goals should be SMART:

- ◆ Specific
- ◆ Measurable
- ◆ Achievable
- ◆ Relevant
- ◆ Time framed

For example, performance criteria for an annual assessment may include specific goals such as: "Maintain guest Comment Card satisfaction ratings that average 4 out of 5"; "Increase average check value per meal by $2.50"; or "Reduce shrinkage level to industry standard of 2%".

> ➤ Personal development needs (training, seminars, etc.). There are more training programs for tourism workers than ever before, and managers should become familiar with what is available in their area. Giving employees access to new training is a worthwhile investment; performance and service levels will improve in addition to employee satisfaction.

> ➤ It is important to foster an innovation culture, where employees put forward proposals that have the potential to improve products, services, and processes. Scheduling regular meetings during which staff members are encouraged to put forth their ideas not only creates a positive company culture, but can also result in productivity improvements.

RETENTION

Keeping good employees satisfied so that they remain in their positions is an important goal. Some industry experts estimate that it can cost up to 18 months' salary to replace a management-level staff member, and up to six months' salary to replace front-line staff. A 2003 report from British Columbia shows that more than half of new workers in the tourism industry leave their jobs within one year; although the seasonality of the business accounts for some of this, employees cite under-appreciation as a key reason for their departure.[2]

Tourism operators must be aware of the need to develop a service-oriented corporate culture, and to build performance and reward systems around it. New employees take time going up a learning curve to become familiar with the operations-specific details of the business; however, when a service focus suffuses every aspect of operations, the longer an employee stays with the company, the greater their value.

Managers must learn to value employees not only for their knowledge of "how things run", but for their fit within the company's service culture as well. Further, productivity is directly linked to retention; in companies with high turnover, lower productivity is the norm. "Studies from the Gallup organization show that employees who have an above-average attitude toward their work will generate 38 percent higher customer satisfaction scores, 22 percent higher productivity, and 27 percent higher profits for their companies."[3]

When your company is lucky enough to have high-performing employees who meet the goals of the company in both production and service standards, reward systems must be in place to make it attractive for these stars to remain with your firm. As discussed above, offering a competitive compensation package and a motivating environment are critical. Tying performance to longer-range goals that measure success for your particular firm is also important.

The economy has experienced diverse upheavals during the last two decades, but one fact that will not change is the shrinking of the labour pool. Competition for qualified and talented people will only become worse in the years to come. "Both the U.S. Census Bureau and a report from Andersen Consulting indicate that the workforce will begin to experience a negative growth rate beginning in the year 2015."[4] Taking the time to develop effective retention strategies is no longer a luxury, but a necessity.

HUMAN RESOURCES PLANNING

Short and mid-term planning involves the assessment of workforce requirements to handle pressing operational tasks. Longer-term (strategic) planning involves a forward-looking analysis of HR needs to meet the company's growth requirements. Both processes involve:

> Managing growth or market contraction issues. The seasonal nature of many tourism businesses makes planning particularly important.

> Anticipating product or service migrations.

> Assessing the type of employees required.

> Establishing future compensation, training and staff development initiatives.

Effective human resources planning requires managers to first familiarize themselves with current employment legislation. Different legislation can apply for different categories of workers, i.e. full time, part time, seasonal, contractors, resident managers. Safety regulation is another area that managers must familiarize themselves with. As well, each province has its own employment and labour standards, although each generally covers the following areas:

> Minimum wage
> Pay days
> Deductions
> Overtime and hours of work
> Leave (parental, medical, compassionate)
> Statutory holidays
> Vacation
> Meal Breaks
> Termination

The degree of complexity in employment law has risen in recent years (along with employees' own knowledge of it): company owners need to understand this aspect of their business very well, and should not hesitate to seek professional advice when necessary.

Next, an audit should be done of the company's overall human resources needs – and this should be updated regularly as the company grows and new directions/activities/ priorities are identified.

Further planning would then include the development of job descriptions for each employee, as well as performance criteria for their areas of responsibility. As mentioned previously, industry standards have been developed for many tourism job descriptions, and various templates for performance evaluations are also available from HR consultants or other government resources.

2. Leadership

The following leadership issues and requirements need to be considered in managing a small- or medium-sized business:

Organizational Structure

Smaller companies experience continuous organizational and management challenges as they grow. Many of these business owners are generalists and often lack, or cannot afford, qualified professional staff.

The stages in the organizational life of a typical small business can be summarized as follows:

Level One: is a one-person operation who does everything.

Level Two: the owner becomes a player/coach and participates extensively in all facets of the business.

Level Three: the owner has hired an intervening layer of management (typically sales and production managers).

Level Four: the management functions are more formalized with more control processes put into place.

Figure 6-1 (below) illustrates a simple functional organization chart that could be applied to Level Two or Level Three businesses. The earlier the growth stage, the more likely one person will assume more than one functional role.

Figure 6-1 Functional Organization Chart

A Functional Organizational Chart

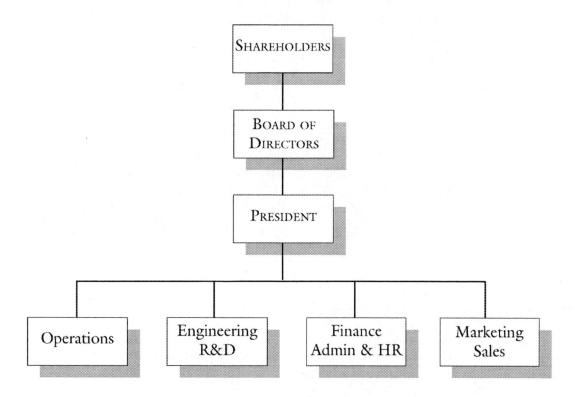

SKILLS DEVELOPMENT

Developing the following leadership skills will result in a more proactive and effective management team:

> ➤ Listening skills: active listening involves looking at issues from others' perspectives and also understanding and learning from them.

> ➤ MBWA (Management By Walking Around): communicating with and listening to employees at all levels of the company.

> ➤ Mentoring: developing employees for future growth through constructive feedback and teaching.

> Empowerment: strengthening employee beliefs in their own effectiveness. This can be accomplished by ensuring that authority and decision making are progressively pushed to lower and lower levels. Employees are encouraged to embark on reasonable initiatives without fear of retribution.

> Motivation: two concepts that are sometimes considered:

> '360 degree feedback'. This process is also known as 'full-circle-feedback'. This process involves gathering observations about performance from supervisors, peers, subordinates and, sometimes customers, and then linking this feedback to the employee's own self evaluation. The intent is to obtain as much frank feedback from as many perspectives as possible. Concerns with this type of review systems include:

> ♦ Anonymous reviews from staff or colleagues may use the system to settle old scores.
> ♦ The process can be extremely time-consuming.

> Open book management. All employees receive relevant information about the company's financial performance and condition. This is often tied to profit sharing and/or stock ownership plans. This process also helps employees see the necessity for change, which is invariably driven by financial realities. It also builds trust so everyone can see what is going on and where the company is headed.

Teams and Teamwork

Within many organizations, employees are teaming up and partnering to solve complex issues under tight time constraints.

Trends and Observations

> Teams are now replacing the boss-employee coupling of the past.

> Teams today are being formed to maximize competitive advantage. The size of the team depends on the scope of the process involved.

> Teams can be functional (e.g., sales teams organized by geography) or cross-functional (e.g., engineers and sales people working together in the launch of a new product).

> Effective team performance takes time to achieve. Harnessing the team's 'collective intelligence' can be a challenge when trust or agenda issues surface.

> ➤ Teams fail when their team members are more concerned with individual agendas versus the common goals of the group.

> ➤ Indications of trouble within teams are extreme polarization or a total absence of conflict. Note: Some disagreement is considered healthy.

An entire body of knowledge has developed in business research that examines team dynamics and how companies can maximize team synergies, and avoid the productivity losses that can happen when teams aren't working well. Training in style analysis and conflict management techniques can be very valuable for managers who supervise teams of employees.

For tourism companies, front line delivery staff can face particular stress: customers can be demanding, rude, and even abusive. Managers need to recognize that these situations can be emotionally exhausting, demoralizing and psychologically overwhelming for their staff members. In firms that encourage a team approach, having an interactive culture where coworkers consistently support and collaborate with one another can go a long way towards alleviating the possibility of "service burnout".

MANAGEMENT CAPABILITIES

Many owners and managers of growing companies 'don't know what they don't know'.

We have prepared the following 'prescriptions' for effective management and leadership. These will allow the reader to assess his or her own capabilities:

> ➤ Have you been able to identify your company's key success factors? Can you describe them in a succinct fashion?

> ➤ Have you established close and trusting relationships with your key stakeholders (employees, customers, suppliers, shareholders, investors)?

> ➤ Is a high standard of ethics and integrity maintained? Do your people know what you stand for?

> ➤ Do you possess strong functional management skills in the finance, marketing, operations, HR, technology, and strategic planning areas?

> ➤ Assess your level of competence. Someone once said that in calm waters, every ship has a good captain. Being competent, especially from a managerial perspective, involves a complete understanding of your business.

> ➤ Do you give credit where credit is due? Selflessness is an important quality.

➤ Have you been able to create an understandable and compelling vision for the company that is anchored by an appropriate organizational structure for your competitive environment?

➤ Has the vision and strategic direction been clearly communicated?

➤ Are you able to instill and inspire confidence among your employees to take on challenging tasks and assignments?

➤ Do you encourage risk and invite dissent from your people? Have they cultivated a sense of urgency and awareness that they need to contribute more than they cost?

➤ Do you emphasize flexibility and the development of skill-sets that allow employees to work across departmental boundaries?

➤ Are you maintaining a broad perspective by continually asking:

➤ What if...? Why do we do this...? What will it take...?

For managers of smaller companies, the number of day-to-day tasks can seem especially overwhelming, and attention to personal development as a leader – including the ability to think in big-picture terms – is often relegated to the back burner.

It is important, therefore, that managers make the time to regularly get away from the environment of their day-to-day duties, to connect with others who can offer ideas and advice, or different perspectives on management challenges.

Joining industry associations, attending conferences, and connecting with the local Chamber of Commerce or Rotary will afford good opportunities both for professional development and personal growth. Similarly, hiring professionals for accounting or legal advice can also give additional access to information about industry trends.

Managers might also consider investing in the short-term services of a professional coach. By offering objective analysis and feedback on performance and leadership styles, a good business coach can help a manager see what they themselves may have been missing, including decisions, traits, or preferences which may be holding back a company's growth or efficiency.

BOARDS OF DIRECTORS

The benefits derived from establishing an effective Board of Directors can include:

- ➤ A competent and active Board of Directors is critical to the capital raising process and company credibility. Board members will often be appointed by early-stage investors in the company.

- ➤ The Board ensures that management has developed and implemented a realistic business and strategic plan.

- ➤ Independence and objectivity is provided by outside directors versus using family members, paid professionals or senior management.

- ➤ Carefully selected Board members can provide valuable expertise and contacts that will assist the company's growth.

SOME ALTERNATIVES:

- ➤ An increased focus on a director's legal responsibilities and liability sometimes makes it difficult to attract talented Board members. A Board of Advisors (or Advisory Board) can be set up, consisting of a similar group of independent and qualified individuals.

   Note: A key difference is that the actions of the members are only advisory with the result their personal liability will be reduced. However, appointees should carefully review the terms of their engagement with their corporate lawyer.

- ➤ For earlier stage companies, the development of a mentor network can be a time saving and cost-effective strategy. Mentors can often be accessed through local Chamber of Commerce and technology associations. Retired or semi-retired legal, accounting, commercial banking or consulting professionals can be an excellent source of informal guidance and feedback.

Useful Web Sites:

www.inc.com	Inc web site – excellent HR information section
www.cthrc.ca	Canadian Tourism Human Resource Council
www.go2hr.ca	Go2 The Resource for People in Tourism
www.coach.net	Information and access to professional coaching services

Endnotes

1. Lovelock, Christopher H., *Managing Services: Marketing, Operations and Human Resources, 2nd Edition.* Prentice Hall, New Jersey, 1992, pp. 228.

2. *Recruit, Retain & Train: Developing a Super, Natural Tourism Workforce in British Columbia.* British Columbia Tourism Human Resources Development Task Force, 2003.

3. Smith, Gregory P. *Here Today, Here Tomorrow: Transforming Your Workforce from High-Turnover to High-Retention.* Dearborn Trade, 2001, pp. ii

4. Smith, website introduction:
   http://www.chartcourse.com/heretodayintro.html.

CHAPTER 7
THE TECHNOLOGY ASSESSMENT

OVERVIEW

For the tourism sector, information and communication technology has had a tremendous impact on the way that companies do business. Consumers have ready access to an overwhelming amount of information regarding any travel or tourism experience that they might be considering. Travel and tourism products have become the most common items bought and sold over the Internet, and this is only one application of technology which has had transformational effects. Highlighted below are specific applications.

TRANSPORTATION

Looking further back, the upgrading of international transportation systems has been the result of consistent technological improvements, not only in global reservation systems and access to new destinations through pioneering computer technologies such as Sabre and Amadeus, but also in the very means by which we reach our destination. Automobiles, tour buses, trains, cruise ships and aircraft have all enjoyed significant improvements over time, making it more and more comfortable for travelers to get from one place to another. The process of traveling has become more appealing as a result of these technological improvements.

RESERVATIONS

Changes to our media systems have also impacted the tourism sector. With improvements in communications systems, live coverage of events as they happen around the world has become the norm. Anyone can "experience" the excitement of events happening in any corner of the globe – such as the Olympics or the Millennium celebrations – thus raising the appeal of featured destinations for future travel consideration. It no longer takes a word-of-mouth recommendation, or a trip to our local travel agent, to gain exposure to potential travel destinations. The entire world is shared with us every day through television, newspapers, and other media.

Internet

Of course, the biggest technological impact on the tourism sector has been the widespread adoption of the Internet. The rise of online distributors of tourism products has enabled tourism operators to access a worldwide consumer base, while selling unused products at deep discounts on line helps to balance the high perishability of many tourism products (hotel rooms, airline seats). A recent US study of travelers …

"… reveals the majority (91%) want to comparison shop multiple hotel brands when booking a hotel. According to the Orbitz Hotel Survey, conducted online by Harris Interactive®, nearly half of consumers (49%) believe web sites like Orbitz offer the lowest hotel rates more than calling hotels directly (25%) or using hotel websites (22%) do. Amid industry discussion on where consumers find the best hotel deals, with online agencies or through hotels directly, the survey found that over the next 12 months, more online travelers (43%) anticipate using third-party sites like Orbitz most frequently for hotel reservations than calling a hotel directly (40%) or using hotel websites (35%)."[1]

Distribution

As the use of global distribution systems expands and industry standards are adopted, tourism operators are encouraged to shop carefully for partners that best meet their needs. A distributor's performance statistics should be examined closely, and operators need to determine whether that distributor can assist in accessing particular target markets. This potential partner should be able to work with your own reservation system, and payment transfers should be made promptly and seamlessly. The company should also allow you to maintain full control over pricing and inventory management. There are enough distributors in today's market that it should not be difficult to find the partners that will provide the most benefits to your particular organization.

Business Systems

On a corporate level, a variety of technology-based business systems have also had an impact on productivity and quality management. In many cases, investing in new technology provides a high return on investment (ROI) not only from increased revenues, but also from cost savings gained by considerably reducing employee effort in performing certain tasks.

Point of Sale

Retail and food and beverage point of sale (POS) systems can contribute a great deal to inventory management and purchasing. Systems are now available that can track sales in real time, and produce reports automatically, in custom formatting, that can aid in decision making at numerous levels. Capacity and yield management can be closely tied to revenue management when data is up to date and presented in the most effective format. For companies with more than one location, comparing data against a variety of factors can leverage the particular circumstances of each branch to ensure the highest efficiencies. For hotel or club operations, POS systems can also be tied into customer relationship management, to enable a higher level of service based on understanding clients' histories and preferences down to the last detail.

QUALITY MANAGEMENT

A number of systems can also help with overall quality management for tourism operators. Rapid response systems for guest requests, preventive maintenance, guestroom management, quality inspections, guest recognition programs, and guest comment tracking are all important factors of quality management, and technological solutions exist for all of these areas.

SECURITY

Another critical area in which technological advances have had a positive impact is security. Physical security systems for guestrooms and other property areas, as well as the protection of data gathered for customer relationship management (CRM) purposes, and even the security of company websites for on-line purchasing, have all been transformed by new technology in recent years. Given the litigious nature of operating in today's hospitality environment, keeping up to date in the protection of your company and your guests is a worthwhile investment.

MARKETING

New initiatives have also changed the way that tourism operators compete for conference and group meeting clients. Hoteliers and meeting planners are now using automatic Request For Proposal (RFP) generation for space requirements, precisely outlining the exact conditions of the event. With full information provided, in a pre-determined format, hotels can provide the best possible service to meeting planners that use their facilities. On-line registration for event attendees can further enhance efficiency, by allowing for instant sharing of data on registrations, and effective management of guest room allocation. Marketing opportunities are also provided by on-line registration, whereby hotels can offer special deals to attendees, or highlight certain products and services that they offer.

SELF SERVICE SOLUTIONS

Self-service solutions form another area of technology enhancements that have been embraced by the tourism sector. In addition to the airline check-in kiosks that have become quite common in our airports, other means of self service have been introduced that save tourism operators time and money: interactive television systems in hotels, and web-based check-in services for both airlines and hotels are examples of new technologies that are being adopted more and more frequently. In British Columbia, the Vancouver International Airport Authority was recently presented with a Technology in Tourism Award for this very approach: the development and implementation of a web-based passenger check-in application specifically for cruise ship passengers. The new system resulted in much shorter processing times for cruise ship passengers, which thereby reduced airport congestion and made for a more streamlined client experience.

IMPLEMENTATION

Tourism operators who are considering the implementation of new technology solutions should ensure that they undertake sufficient research before making purchases. Talk to other operators, and ask detailed questions about their satisfaction with their choices. Research the background of the solution provider and ask for references from within the tourism sector. Once a choice has been made, be sure to schedule a post-implementation assessment. Has the new technology created a competitive advantage? Has it resulted in productivity improvement, or higher profits? If not, will the service provider work with you to make changes that will better meet your needs?

In cases where you are considering working closely with technology solutions providers, it is helpful to understand as much as possible about their operations. The following detailed assessment process provides some insights as to technology companies' potential and their challenges. Tourism operators can use this assessment process to help determine, in essence, how long a potential technology solution provider might be around. This assessment consists of the following areas:

1. Technology description
2. Products/services and processes
3. Intellectual property issues
4. Markets
5. Potential risk factors

Investment and pay-back considerations would normally be incorporated into such an assessment process; however, these issues are dealt with in more detail in Chapter Nine.

1. TECHNOLOGY DESCRIPTION

Consider:

> ➢ What is the technology and the opportunity? Can this be summarized to a stranger in an elevator within 30 seconds? If not, develop a 30-second message.

> ➢ What is the development stage? Technology push or market pull?

Technology 'pushers': are the developers and inventors who enthusiastically push and promote their new technology although their products and markets have yet to be clearly identified. Once the markets are identified, they attempt to push even harder!

Market 'pullers': are completely familiar with a given market and have identified the need for a product. They then set out to pull their product through a technology development process.

These relationships are illustrated in Figure 7-1 (below). To quote Denzil Doyle, in *Making Technology Happen*, ask the following simple question, "What is the product and how much of it can be sold?"

Figure 7-1 Technology Push versus Pull

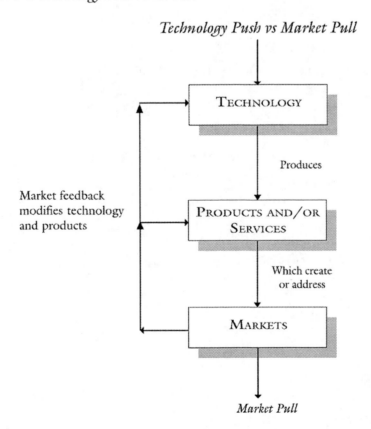

Technology Push vs Market Pull

2. PRODUCTS/SERVICES AND PROCESSES

Consider:

> What is the purpose of the product or service?

> Does it meet potential customer needs?

> What are the unique features? Cost, design, simplicity?

> What is the estimated technological life?

> At what stage is the product on the innovation chain?

   1. Ideas: Tend to be easy to generate and easy to kill.

   2. R&D: Technical stage or market stage?

   3. Development: Engineering prototype, pilot run, client evaluations.

   4. Production: Product testing and refinements.

   5. Market development: Beta testing, setting up distribution channels.

> What type of production processes will be employed?

> capital intensive

> labor intensive

> material intensive

> Is there a product migration (follow-on) product strategy?

Consider that:

> One product technology companies are often doomed to failure.

> 'Follow on' products will ideally consist of two new additions to the product family:

   i) one with a lower price and lower functionality.

   ii) one with a higher price and higher functionality.

> An effective product migration strategy will lead to timely product introductions so that new products generate revenues at the same time as older ones are reaching maturity or starting to decline.

3. INTELLECTUAL PROPERTY ISSUES

Safeguarding intellectual property is a complex yet essential task for technology companies. The status of a company's intellectual property (IP) is a key area of focus and due diligence by potential investors.

The following brief review highlights the various types of IP protection:

A) PATENTS

- A patent does *not* grant an individual exclusive rights to an invention. The patent is granted to the inventor who is first to file an application. In the U.S. it is the first to invent.

- The inventor is granted a 'negative right' under the law and is able to exclude others from using and making the invention. This right is granted in exchange for making the patent information known to the public.

- In Canada, present patent legislation grants the owner the legal right to exclude others from using the patentable invention for 20 years from the date of filing. Patents are <u>not</u> renewable once the 20-year time period has elapsed. (In the USA, a 20-year period has also been established).

KEY QUESTIONS TO ASK PRIOR TO IMPLEMENTING A PATENT STRATEGY:

Is there an existing or potential market for the invention?

What are the costs to manufacture and market the invention?

Is funding in place to commercially exploit the invention?

REQUIREMENTS FOR A PATENT

i) **Utility:** Does the device or process have a practical benefit that meets customer needs?

ii) **Novelty:** The invention has to be new.

Note: If the invention has been publicly disclosed, developed, or sold more than one year prior to a Canadian or USA patent application, the patent application will be denied.

iii) **Inventive ingenuity:** The invention must be 'non obvious'. It must be an improvement or development that is not obvious to anyone possessing average skill in the technology field.

The registration process

- ➤ Preliminary search: usually carried out in the Canadian and USA patent offices. A broader and more comprehensive 'infringement search' can also be completed to see if the invention infringes another patent.

- ➤ Preparation and filing of the application: Use an experienced patent lawyer or agent to guide you through this complex process.

- ➤ The registration process involves drafting an application that:

  - ♦ clearly distinguishes your invention from previous ones; and

  - ♦ defines specific claims which establish the scope and quality of the patent.

Acceptance or Rejection

If accepted, the patent holder has the legal right to exclude others from using, making, or selling the invention at the date of approval. It should be noted that up to three years can often elapse from the initial application, due to the considerable volume of patent applications currently being filed.

B) Patent Pending

This status can be placed or affixed to a device or process after filing the patent application and prior to registration. It has no legal effect. It serves to warn others and, in some ways, can offer more protection than if the patent had been formally accepted. The invention details are not revealed by the government to outsiders for the period of time during the application process. Potential competitors may be deterred from copying for fear of infringing on the forthcoming patent.

C) Trade Secrets

An alternative to patents. Non disclosure (the invention is kept as a trade secret) – this could sometimes be more valuable than the benefits of patent protection because trade secrets have an indefinite term and do not involve any disclosure.

D) TRADEMARKS

- ➤ Trademarks are any name, symbol, or expression which an individual or organization uses to distinguish its products or services.

- ➤ In Canada, the first person to use a trademark is entitled to register the mark and obtain exclusive rights. The trademark is registered for 15 years from the date of registration and is renewable.

Benefits in registering trademarks include:

- ➤ Alerts others of its existence.

- ➤ Provides nation-wide protection.

- ➤ Allows a holder to commence trademark infringement proceedings.

E) COPYRIGHT

- ➤ Copyright protection provides artists/authors with the sole right to transmit, reproduce, sell and distribute their work or to permit someone else to do so.

- ➤ Protection lasts for the author's lifetime plus 50 years after the author's death.

- ➤ In Canada, copyright is automatically conferred upon the creator of an original work without registration.

- ➤ Registration is voluntary but advisable. This step provides the owner with a basis to commence a copyright infringement action if required.

F) INDUSTRIAL DESIGN

- ➤ Can be registered for a single term of 10 years.

- ➤ Prevents other firms from directly copying a design.

- ➤ Protects the design of a functional device or object.

- ➤ Additional intellectual property rights are available within specific industries.

G) CONFIDENTIALITY AND EMPLOYMENT AGREEMENTS

> ➤ Essential for an organization to protect its technology by ensuring that outsiders and key employees have signed and are legally bound by written agreements.

H) ACCESS RESTRICTIONS

> ➤ To production, laboratory research facilities, data storage areas. This process should also include a disaster recovery plan (fire, flood, earthquake).

COMPLETION OF AN INTELLECTUAL PROPERTY PLAN

Steps:

> ➤ Complete an Intellectual Property (IP) audit to identify and inventory IP assets. The process includes a review of records management, confidentiality practices, and contracts administration.

> ➤ Analyze IP strengths and weaknesses. Decide what technologies to develop and ask, "Is leadership in these technologies affordable?" Can you "license in" some outside technological processes?

> ➤ Ensure inventors are product driven. Company engineers should file patents as an ongoing and integral part of product development. They should also complete patent infringement searches as part of the pre-design process.

> ➤ Develop a budget for patent costs.

> ➤ Initiate an IP training program for key employees.

4. MARKETS

Technology companies often attempt to market their products or services based on technical abilities rather than satisfying customer needs. Consider the following questions:

> ➤ Have you assessed your market potential in relation to total market size?

> ➤ What is your expected market penetration and market share?

➤ Assess replacement versus incremental markets?

   1. Replacement sales are those that involve the replacement of existing units. Buyers are normally influenced by price or increased quality.

   2. Incremental sales are those made to 'early adopters and visionaries' who are influenced by product functionality and newness versus price.

➤ Understand your distribution channels. Are distribution agreements mutually advantageous?

➤ Has a detailed marketing plan been completed, identifying target market segments?

LICENSING OPPORTUNITIES

If a technology process is initiated and is not suitable for development into a discrete product or service, can it be licensed for use in other operations? Some benefits of licensing:

➤ Licensees (receiving the technology) have existing products or facilities and are able to acquire the technology more cheaply and quickly than by completing their own R&D process.

➤ The licenser is able to exploit its technology in secondary markets without large marketing and production expenditures.

➤ Licensing is an effective way to test and develop offshore markets.

➤ Licensees are unlikely to become future competitors.

5. POTENTIAL RISK FACTORS

Some key questions to consider:

➤ Is there a threat of emerging new competitors and/or superior technology?

➤ How short are your product life-cycles with resulting obsolescence issues?

➤ What is the relationship between the stage of technology development and cash flow generation?

Figure 7-2 (next page) illustrates the often painful process in completing product development while experiencing severe cash flow constraints.

Figure 7-2 Technology evolution and cash flow realities

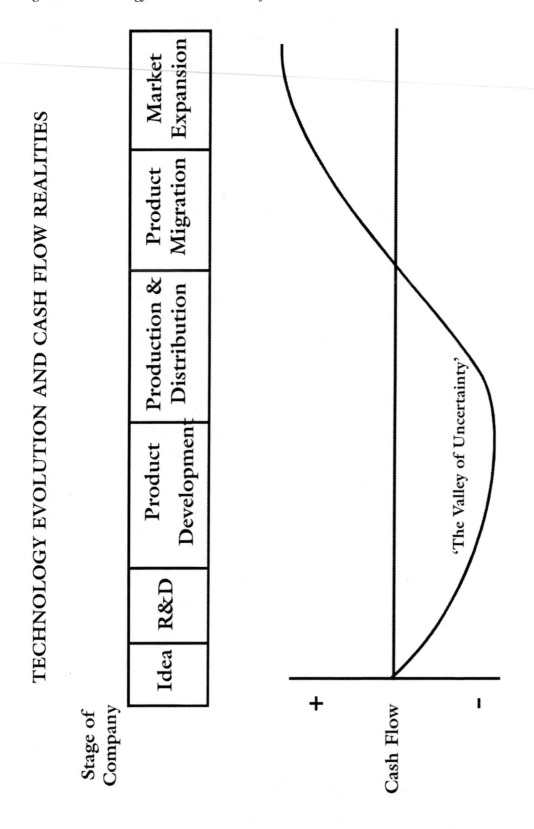

➤ The negative cash flow experienced during the earlier stages of product development, along with unexpected expenditure surprises, can lead to feelings of despair in the 'valley of uncertainty'. As operations ramp up to meet market demand, cash flow shortfalls begin to diminish, leading to increasing optimism.

➤ How mobile are key employees and management? Is there potential to lose intellectual property 'walking out of the door'? Can this be counteracted by stock option incentives (handcuffs) and/or non-compete agreements?

➤ Are there growth-related risks? What would be the impact be on:

  ♦ production?

  ♦ human resources?

  ♦ finances?

➤ Is there a dependence on a limited number of customers?

➤ Is there a dependence on a limited number of suppliers? Are there alternative sources of supply or does the potential to outsource exist?

➤ How strong are your proprietary rights? Is there potential for infringement lawsuits?

➤ Is there a currency or foreign receivable risk? Can these be hedged or insured by the Export Development Corporation (EDC)?

➤ Do you have the financial resources to cover ongoing R&D costs that are necessary for product enhancements and the development of new generation technologies?

➤ Do you have the ability to raise additional capital via committed investors with deep pockets?

USEFUL WEB SITES:

www.ipmall.fplc.edu/	Intellectual property mall – Franklin Pierce
www.redherring.com	Red Herring – business of technology
www.hospitalityupgrade.com	On-line version of magazine for technology in hospitality sector.
http://itt.ec3.at	Information Technology & Tourism Journal
www.ifitt.org	International Federation for IT and Travel & Tourism
www.traveldailynews.com	Travel newsletter that features a technology section

Endnotes

1. New Orbitz survey finds travelers prefer to book with online agencies, August 27, 2004. http://www.traveldailynews.com/new.asp?newid=18207&subcategory_id=77

SECTION 3

THE COMPANY LIFE-CYCLE AND RELATED FUNDING INITIATIVES

CHAPTER 8
NEW BUSINESS OPPORTUNITIES AND STRATEGIES

OVERVIEW

This chapter deals with the first stage of evolution that tourism business owners encounter – the new business opportunity. The following key areas will be reviewed:

1. Self assessment
2. The start-up process
3. Buying an existing business
4. Valuation issues
5. Buying a franchise operation
6. Entering a family business
7. Characteristics of successful new business ventures

1. SELF ASSESSMENT

We have developed a two-stage check list which will permit an aspiring entrepreneur to critically assess his or her ability to succeed in their new business endeavor.

A. THE PROPOSED BUSINESS VENTURE

Some key questions to consider:

> Do you have the necessary experience and knowledge to operate the business?

> Do you have any practical experience in sales, marketing, finance, or human resource management?

> Will the venture actually be a "job disguised as a business"?

> Does the business have the potential to reward you for your time, effort, hard work and sleepless nights?

> Will there be future opportunities to expand or diversify the business?

> Who are the customers and clients who will be using your products or services?

> How easily could a potential competitor start a similar business?

> How much control will suppliers (materials and labor) have?

> How many employees are required? What level and types of compensation are necessary?

> Do you have an experienced accountant, lawyer, and commercial banker in place?

> Who will take over if something happens to you? Do you have a succession plan in place?

B. YOUR PERSONAL RESOURCES AND CHARACTERISTICS

> Are you willing to risk your savings in this venture? Does the opportunity involve additional personal debt?

> Do you have the commitment of your family? Is spousal or a secondary source of income available to support you?

> How long could your family accept a temporary drop in income?

> Do you have strong leadership and decision-making skills?

> Are you able to set priorities and keep to them?

> Do you have a strong work ethic, undeterred by long hours and lost weekends?

➤ Are you able to make carefully rationalized decisions and then stick with them?

➤ Are you in good health and able to maintain high levels of activity?

2. THE START-UP

Starting a tourism business from scratch is a complex and challenging exercise. The following steps describe the process:

A. THE OPPORTUNITY

➤ To what extent is there a 'window of opportunity' to exploit your idea, product, or service? What is the potential size of the market? How fast can the market grow?

➤ Will the potential earnings be sufficient to provide an acceptable return on your capital and time? Are the earnings sustainable?

➤ Does the proposed product or service meet a tangible and, likely, urgent need?

➤ Could this opportunity lead to additional avenues for market expansion or product diversification?

B. DEFINING THE BUSINESS STRATEGY

➤ Are barriers to entry in place or can they be easily created to deter emerging competition? (Example: the early registration of trademarks or copyrights.)

➤ Have market segments and target clients been identified and researched? What distribution channels are available to access these customers?

➤ Supplier power: Are you dependent on a few suppliers who control critical inputs to your proposed product or service?

➤ Buyer power: Will buyers (your future clients) expect pricing concessions as you endeavor to launch your product?

C. EVALUATING AND MAINTAINING RESOURCES

> What personnel, capabilities, and relationships are already in place? Which ones are required in the future?

> What makes the proposed venture unique? Have the necessary proprietary and value-added attributes been protected?

> What are the regulatory and legal requirements associated with running the business?

> Are there adequate financial and operational resources available to overcome unexpected obstacles and setbacks?

> There are various ways to acquire specific resources for the venture. Consider the following:

> - Renting – equipment
> - Leasing – premises
> - Borrowing – funds for working capital
> - Subcontracting – employees

> How will the right employees and supporting professionals be selected?

> What types of incentives need to be offered to your personnel?

> How will the owner's roles and responsibilities be delegated as the company grows?

D. EXIT STRATEGIES

After running a successful business, the owners need to formulate a suitable exit strategy. Exit strategy options include:

> Sale of company to an outside party or employees.

> Acquisition by larger company.

> Public offering (IPO).

> Liquidation: sale of assets, debt repayment, and distribution of proceeds to the owner(s).

3. BUYING A BUSINESS

Use the following four-step check list when deciding whether to buy a business:

A. WHY PURCHASE AN EXISTING BUSINESS?

- Price: the company is being purchased at a price below the estimated costs of starting a new business.

- Track record: uncertainties will be reduced when buying an existing business which already has a proven track record in place.

- Established relationships: will already be in place with clients, suppliers, and work force.

B. HOW DO YOU LOCATE A BUSINESS TO BUY?

The following are some information sources that can assist you in your search process:

- Newspaper and business magazine advertisements.
- Trade journals.
- Business brokers and commercial realtors.
- Trustees and Receivers.
- Local economic development and technology association offices.
- Professional advisors.
- Internet search engines.

C. DUE DILIGENCE — WHY IS THE BUSINESS FOR SALE?

- Lack of succession plans (no apparent heirs).
- Owners' retirement or ill health.
- Owner has other investments or businesses competing for his or her time.

> The business expanded too fast, resulting in depleted cash resources and an inability to attract additional equity capital.

> Partnership problems.

> Lost enthusiasm, reduced commitment, fatigue.

> Specific industry sector has reached maturity or is in decline.

> Local economy and location are weak.

> Competitive pressures.

> Outdated technology infrastructure and systems.

> Potential for litigation.

> Lease renewal is too expensive.

D. THE EVALUATION PROCESS

The following factors influence the selling price of a business:

> *Management:* Assess the quality and performance of existing management.

> *Financing:* How much debt is carried by the business (is there pressure from creditors?)

> Is a *vendor take-back* (VTB) available to assist with the funding of the purchase price?

> *Quality of assets*

   ♦ Accounts receivable – what has been the collection track record?

   ♦ Inventory – any obsolescence issues?

   ♦ Fixed assets -estimated current market value and remaining economic life?

> *Leases*

   ♦ Transferable?

   ♦ Maturity dates?

   ♦ Escalation clauses?

> *Intellectual property assets:* Are there patents or trademarks in place?

> Competition: Is there a potential for big-box competition?

> *Financial history:* Revenue, earnings, cash generation performance?

> *Warranties:* How many have been extended? What is their duration? Is there any potential financial exposure?

> *Legal commitments:* Are there any contingent liabilities, unsettled lawsuits, or any overdue rent payments?

> *Product prices:* Have these been compared to competitor price levels? How does the business gross profit margin compare to industry averages?

4. VALUATION TECHNIQUES
WHAT PRICE DO YOU PAY?

Valuing a business is a complex process and is not an exact science. A brief overview is presented here. It is essential to obtain professional advice (accountant, lawyer and/or chartered business valuator) in structuring a formal purchase agreement for a business.

The following valuation approaches will be considered:

A. Asset valuations

B. Market valuations

C. Cash Flow valuations

D. Earnings valuations

A. ASSET-BASED VALUATION
THERE ARE THREE VARIETIES:

1) *Modified book value:*

Determined by adjusting the book value to reflect the difference between the historical cost and current value of the assets.

Adjustments will be made for any surplus appraisal value on land and buildings, while intangible asset values would be heavily discounted.

2) *Replacement value:* Value is based on the cost to replace the firm's assets.

3) Liquidation value: Value is based on the funds available if a firm was to liquidate its assets.

A weakness to these approaches is that they all fail to recognize the firm as a 'going concern' that generates sustainable revenue and earnings.

B. MARKET-BASED VALUATION

This approach is based on actual market prices of firms that have recently been sold or are trading publicly on a stock exchange.

Calculation:

Price Earnings Ratio = $\dfrac{\text{Market Price}}{\text{After tax earnings}}$

Weaknesses:

- Finding appropriate multiple comparables is difficult.

- Public company data is not likely appropriate given differences in the scale of business operations.

C. CASH FLOW VALUATIONS

A cash flow valuation involves estimating a company's future operating cash flows (EBITDA minus regular capital expenditures) and discounting back to a present value using the investors required rate of return.

This rate of return would be computed by starting with a 'risk free' rate of return (present treasury bill rate) plus a risk premium usually between 10% and 30% depending on the size of the company and associated risk factors. Additionally, the opportunity cost of the invested funds (alternate uses) needs to be considered.

D. EARNINGS-BASED VALUATION

The estimated value of the firm is based on its ability to generate future, sustainable earnings.

Process: Derive an estimate of stabilized earnings by considering:

Historical earnings: Use average earnings for the past five years and adjust for non-recurring revenue or expense items.

Future earnings: Those anticipated under present ownership.

Note: The purchaser may derive a different (higher or lower) future earnings estimate based on efficiencies arising from new management (higher earnings) or restructuring costs (lower earnings) that will have an impact on price negotiations.

A KEY QUESTION — WHAT EARNINGS?

There is considerable debate as to which 'earnings' definition should be used in the earnings valuation calculation. There are three earnings definitions:

1. Earnings after tax: net profit before any allowance for extraordinary items.

2. EBIT: earnings before interest and taxes. Measures the earning power and value of the underlying business without the effects of financing.

3. EBITDA: earnings before interest, taxes, depreciation, and amortization. A more accurate measure of cash flows generated by a business.

For small-to medium-sized businesses, the most realistic valuation technique usually involves EBIT, especially if the financing (interest) effect is not shown.

NEXT STEP: DERIVE A CAPITALIZATION RATE (CAP RATE).

The cap rate can also be presented as a multiple (reciprocal).

Example:

	Cap Rate	Multiple	
Low Risk, Higher Value	20%	5x	100/20
	25%	4x	100/25
Higher Risk, Low Value	33%	3x	100/33

The cap rate selection will be somewhat subjective and is derived from a blend of quantitative and qualitative factors. These include the following:

> P/E ratios of comparable publicly-traded companies.

> Earnings multiples derived from recent company acquisitions in the same industry.

> Industry rules of thumb adjusted for a company's size and track record (internal value factors).

Internal value factors:

- ➤ Financial: Relative strength of balance sheet, absence of intangible assets, and availability of working capital resources.

- ➤ Marketing: A broad, diversified client base, allied with significant penetration into a company's market segment. Unique products or services with the opportunity to increase future sales and earnings.

- ➤ Operations: The capacity of plant and equipment to handle future growth. Flexibility and versatility of machinery to produce new and different products.

It is important to consider surplus assets: i.e., those that do not contribute directly to the company operations. For example, permanent term deposits or a securities portfolio would be added to the capitalized value.

Example: Earnings-based valuation

Company XYZ

- ➤ *Maintainable future earnings (EBIT) per year:* $155,000

  - ◆ Have been derived from the past five years' income statements and adjusted for non-recurring revenue and expense items.

  - ◆ These estimated earnings most likely to be realized in the future under present ownership.

- ➤ *Cap rate/multiple:* 25% (4x)

  - ◆ Equivalent to business risk based on review of current industry multiples (if available) and company's internal value factors.

  - ◆ Will need to meet the purchaser's minimum required rate of return.

- ➤ *Surplus assets – term deposits:* $45,000

VALUATION:

Capitalized earnings	4 x $155,000 =	$620,000
Plus: Surplus assets		$ 45,000
Total estimated value		$665,000

OTHER RELATED ISSUES

Goodwill: the difference between the tangible net worth of the company and the actual purchase price.

Example:

Company book equity	$ 80,000
Purchase price	$140,000
Goodwill	$ 60,000

Goodwill is an intangible asset that will appear on a new company's financial statements. In essence, this 'purchase premium' relates to a basket of intangibles encompassing copyrights, brand name, supplier connections, lease benefits, and location.

The seller will take the position that these intangible factors contribute to earnings generation and, therefore, should have an ascribed value.

A buyer's reluctance to pay a goodwill premium is often mitigated by negotiating an 'earn out' where the vendor takes back financing approximating the agreed value of goodwill. The buyer then pays back the obligation over a negotiated period of time from ongoing company earnings.

PURCHASE OF ASSETS VERSUS SHARES

➤ *Asset Purchase*

♦ The buyer sets up a new corporation and transfers all purchased assets (and property lease, if appropriate) into the new corporation.

♦ The buyer will attempt to allocate:

- a low percentage of the purchase price for goodwill (if any), as tax write-offs are not as attractive for goodwill as for fixed assets.

- a high percentage of the purchase price to depreciable assets, to maximize depreciation deductions in the future.

Note: Assets need to be free and clear of any encumbrances, liens, mortgages and/or security agreements.

➤ *Share Purchase*

♦ The buyer purchases company shares from departing shareholders, and elects his/her own directors and officers.

♦ Debt can be assumed with the vendor receiving the difference between the purchase price and outstanding debt.

♦ Leases, contracts, and licenses typically transfer with the change of share ownership.

♦ Tax losses may be available for the benefit of the buyer.

♦ Past liabilities (direct or contingent) stay with the company and could come back to haunt the new owner.

Which is the best option? It depends on the various benefits accruing to the purchaser and vendor.

The vendor generally wants to take the' share sale' option, benefiting from the $500,000 capital gains deduction available to qualified small business corporations and, at the same time, avoiding any 'recapture' costs associated with an asset sale.

The purchaser usually prefers the 'asset purchase' option in order to take advantage of potential Business Improvement Loan financing for equipment and higher depreciation charges for tax purposes. Also, any unknown problems associated with a share purchase (unattractive contracts and/or employee-related issues) can be avoided.

5. FRANCHISE OPPORTUNITIES

OVERVIEW

A franchise is a special type of partnership where one company (the franchisor) grants the right to sell its products and services to another company or individual (the franchisee).

ADVANTAGES OF FRANCHISING

Franchises are often viewed as a less risky alternative to business ownership.

➤ Lower risk of business failure.

➤ Brand name recognition.

➤ Franchiser support:

- ◆ employee selection/training.
- ◆ inventory control.
- ◆ vendor supplies.
- ◆ lease negotiations.

➤ Financial support:

- ◆ preferential financing packages often including inventory buyback agreements between the franchisor and the franchisee's bank.
- ◆ flexible payment terms to suppliers or product purchases from parent organization.
- ◆ increased purchasing power.
- ◆ additional franchising opportunities to acquire other nearby locations.

FRANCHISING HAZARDS TO AVOID

➤ Excessive up-front franchise fees and ongoing royalty fees (based on a fixed percentage of annual sales which vary from 2% to 15%).

➤ Excessive advertising and promotional fees with a nominal local benefit received.

➤ Growth restrictions: the franchisee is often restricted to a defined sales territory.

➤ Loss of independence: especially painful for those with entrepreneurial orientation.

➤ Encroachment: the franchisor initiates alternate distribution channels (Internet sales, gas station outlets, etc.) that effectively compete with the existing franchisee operation.

➤ Differing legislative protection: protective franchise legislation is usually not in place.

➤ Tired products or services within saturated markets.

➤ Preference to insiders: existing franchisees are offered prime locations before first-time franchise buyers.

➤ Restrictions on sources of supplies.

➤ Restrictions on selling out.

KEY QUESTIONS TO ASK A FRANCHISOR

As part of the due diligence process, ask the following questions:

- How long has the franchise been in business?
- How many franchise outlets are currently in operation?
- How many failures have there been over the past five years? What were the reasons for such failures?
- Is there any litigation in process?
- How many new franchises have been sold over the past five years?
- Does the franchisor have the right to buy out franchisees? How would the price be determined?
- How financially sound is the franchise? Are franchisor financial statements and bank references available?
- How many franchises are operating in the proposed market area?
- Who is the competition?
- What are the fees (upfront, royalty, advertising)? How do these compare to industry averages?
- What support is provided?
  - training
  - lease negotiation
  - financing
  - advertising
  - supplier discounts
  - Are a number of (recent) franchisee references available? (Make contact with them).

6. FAMILY BUSINESS OPPORTUNITIES

Another route to commencing a new venture is the entry to a family-owned business. This opportunity has its own unique characteristics.

Some issues to consider:

> ➤ A key benefit can be the strength of family relationships that often help overcome serious operational setbacks.

> ➤ The founder will invariably leave a deep impact on the culture of the family firm.

> ➤ Changes in culture often occur as leadership passes from one generation to the next.

> ➤ Succession is a key issue. The planning process needs to start early in the successor's life. Tension will invariably develop between the founder and the successor as he/she gains experience.

> ➤ Independent research has shown that there is a lower probability that a third generation will successfully take over the business from the second generation.

7. CHARACTERISTICS OF SUCCESSFUL START-UPS

To conclude this chapter, we leave you with some observations from successful tourism company owners who have survived the new business growth phase.

> ➤ Founders need to have relevant knowledge and experience at the outset (rather than learning the business as they begin operations.)

> ➤ Forge key alliances at an early stage with clients, suppliers, and even competitors (know as "co-petition").

> ➤ Ensure that close management of cash drivers takes place, i.e. prompt account receivable collection, inventory monitoring and advantageous account payable settlement terms.

> ➤ Hire talented people and build a committed team.

> ➤ Stick to what you know.

> ➤ Focus, focus, focus!

- ➤ Develop a strong banking relationship. Keep in touch with your banker on a regular basis.

- ➤ Set your goals high. Think like a public company CEO from Day One.

- ➤ Fully research your competition. Constantly monitor their performance and initiatives.

- ➤ Continually update your management skills.

- ➤ Understand your client market segments and their relative contribution to your gross profit margin.

- ➤ Strive for a comfortable balance between dibt and equity.

- ➤ Assess your ability to survive on a quarterly basis.

USEFUL WEB SITES

www.canadaone.com	Canada One – Small business resource directory
www.cfa.ca	Canadian Franchise Association
www.thebusinesssource.com	Subscription service providing monthly summaries of current business books
www.cbsc.org	Canada Business Service Centers provides information for start-up or existing companies
www.cafeuc.org	Canadian Association of Family Enterprises (CAFÉ)
www.entreworld.org	On-line information for entrepreneurs coded by stages of development

CHAPTER 9
SOURCES OF EQUITY FUNDING

OVERVIEW

Another crucial element in the development of a new business opportunity is securing sufficient funding to grow and maintain the enterprise. This section examines the equity investment process and how it interfaces with the business life cycle. While the orientation of this content is towards technology-based companies, many tourism operators will need to raise equity to successfully launch their business venture. Sources of financing, usually only available once a company has reached a more mature growth phase are examined in detail in Chapter 11.

The stages of a company's development can be categorized as follows:

➤ Seed/Early Stage: Idea generation and proof of concept.

➤ Start Up: Product development, commercialization and some initial marketing.

➤ First Stage: Initial production and sales. Not yet cash flow positive.

➤ Second Stage: Expansion leading to profitable operations and positive cash flow.

➤ Maturity: Product migrations initiated, along with completion of domestic and possibly international expansions.

➤ Additional funding: Obtained from strategic corporate alliances, IPO or M&A (Merger and Acquisition) activities.

➤ Divestment: Outside investors or existing management buy either the company, a division or a product line.

THE EQUITY INVESTMENT PROCESS

1. IDENTIFY FUNDING REQUIREMENTS

Key Points:

- How much cash is required to fund the venture?

- How many dollars will be generated internally (from ongoing cash flows) and how many dollars will be required from external (equity) sources?

- Equity sources will include company founders' cash, grant programs, research tax credits and outside investors.

- How will the funds be allocated?

  - working capital

  - marketing costs

  - capital assets

  - research and development

- When will the funds be advanced? What are the key performance benchmarks or milestones?

- Will the company be able to generate a sufficient rate of return to reward the investors? (Equity investors will typically look for between 25% and 40% annualized returns over a three to five year time horizon.)

  Remember that different investors require different levels of profit sharing, decision making, and management. There must also be an exit strategy established for the investor (an Initial Public Offering (IPO), sale of the company, management buyback, etc.)

- Be aware of the 20/60/20 rule:

  - 20% are winners

  - 60% are the 'living dead'

  - 20% do not survive

2. DEMONSTRATE INVESTMENT POTENTIAL

It is critical to understand the risk assessment process that an equity investor will undertake. The following criteria are usually considered:

- ➤ What is the company's market opportunity? Are there unique product/service features?

- ➤ Is the industry segment attractive to the investor?

- ➤ Is there evidence of a critical need (and customer acceptance) for the product or service?

- ➤ What are the terms of the investment?

- ➤ What percentage of the company is being sold (usually under 50% for early-stage companies because the investor does not want to assume day-to-day operational control and associated headaches).

- ➤ What is the estimated value of the business? How was the value derived? How many other investors are at the table?

- ➤ Sophisticated investors will be looking to 'add value' to the company, aside from their investment of capital. They may have business contacts or knowledge of potential strategic partnerships that could assist the company in achieving its growth objectives.

- ➤ How will return on investment (ROI) requirements be met?

- ➤ Will the investor be able to build a solid and enduring relationship with the target company and its management?

- ➤ What is the historical and projected operating performance and financial structure?

- ➤ Are Intellectual Property interests protected? What other barriers to entry are in place?

- ➤ What is the caliber of the management team? What are the specific management skills and attributes in place now and those required for the future?

- ➤ Is there a viable exit strategy (three to five years) down the road?

- ➤ Is there a Business and Strategy plan in place?

- ➤ How is the investment to be monitored and controlled? (Examples: Board seat, financial statement reporting requirements, capital expenditure approvals, etc.)

3. Complete a Written Investment Proposal

Such a proposal will be built on the primary components of the company business plan, but will be tailored to the equity investment initiative.

Focus should be on the investor's needs and requirements.

Key areas to emphasize:

➤ The market opportunity.

➤ Your management track record (credibility and experience).

➤ Equity stake available to the investor:

- ◆ terms/duration
- ◆ voting rights
- ◆ management control

➤ Revenue/earnings growth projections (to meet investor's ROI).

➤ Anticipated exit strategies for the investor.

➤ Obtain feedback from outside professional advisors.

➤ Ensure confidentiality.

➤ Ensure compliance with all legal and regulatory requirements.

A useful document to accomplish this step is a Business Opportunity Document (BOD) which is a concise two- to three-page summary that describes the investor opportunity. This concept is covered in greater detail in Chapter 13 – Business and Strategic Plans.

4. Identify Potential Investors

The following categories of equity investor can be identified, beginning with the earliest players that come to the table:

➤ **Founder's cash**

Personal cash injections from savings accounts, securities, home equity sources, etc.

➤ **Friends and family (F & F)**

Also known as love money, seed money or guilt money.
Dollar amounts are generally small (up to $100,000), with proceeds typically used to test concepts, initiate product development, and market research.

➤ **Angel investors**

Angels are generally individuals who maintain a low profile and are usually contacted through professional advisors.

These are sophisticated investors who will complete extensive due diligence, with initial investment amounts in the $50,000 to $750,000 range. They typically look for 10 x ROI (Return on Investment) within three to five years (i.e., 20%-35% compounded annual returns).

Angels will usually bring experience, contacts and strategic advice to the table. They are more likely to become involved in an earlier stage company or a regional (versus global) opportunity.

➤ **Government-backed programs**

Some examples:

The Business Development Bank (BDC) provides a spectrum of quasi-equity programs ranging from $100,000 to $1 million for expansion and market development projects that usually require some form of equity matching.

The Industrial Research Assistance Program (IRAP): This program provides match-funding grants (50:50) through the National Research Council.

➤ **Venture capital firms**

Venture capital firms sometimes work with new startups but are more likely to seek out existing companies that need assistance in ramping up revenue and achieving positive cash flow generation. These investors will be professionals with extensive experience and contacts, looking for annualized returns in the following ranges:

- ◆ Start Up: 40%+
- ◆ Expansion: 30%

Investment size normally ranges from $500,000 to $5 million.

These firms tend to 'travel in herds' and will often syndicate to achieve relative safety in numbers. Scalability is important to this type of investor. A business that is able to add new clients with little extra effort and cost is said to be scalable.

➤ **Institutional investors**

Provide equity to medium-sized businesses with investment requirements usually in the $10 million+ range.

Example: Bank subsidiaries (i.e., TD Capital)

> ## Strategic Corporate investors

These investors consist of strategic alliances or corporate partnerships involving established, successful companies that are looking to gain new product and market access or exposure to new technologies.

> ## Public Offerings

Initial Public Offerings (IPOs) involve raising additional capital through a formalized share offering process on public exchanges. In Canada, public exchanges include Toronto, Montreal and CDNX. In the USA, there are 'over the counter' exchanges or NASDAQ.

This process usually takes place after a number of 'private rounds' of equity investments. Timing is crucial from both the investment climate (external) and the company's (internal) cash generation performance. Further dilution of the founding shareholder's interests will take place, along with a new accountability to other stakeholders such as public shareholders, regulators, etc.

A prospectus, available to public shareholders, provides a detailed description of the company and the investment opportunity. Regulators provide tight control over the process to protect the public. Underwriters sell the stock through the selected stock market after deciding on the issue price based upon orders booked from retail and institutional investors.

The process is very expensive and requires a huge time and financial commitment. There will be substantial accounting requirements prior to the IPO that need to be met. The listing process will entail costs between 6-8% of the issue which will be retained by the underwriters. Intensive road shows and lengthy investor relations initiatives add to the overall cost.

One unexpected outcome arising from an IPO is that suppliers, customers and competition suddenly have a detailed update on your financial performance (historical and projected) and your strategic plans by way of the prospectus that is issued to potential investors.

If the IPO process is successful, there will be significant gains in credibility, access to international capital markets and the ability to offer more liquid stock options to attract top-tier employees. However, given the complexity of the process, it is crucial to ask this question a number of times … is the company ready to go public?

RESOURCES AVAILABLE TO LOCATE INVESTORS:

- ➤ Directories or Associations (Canadian Venture Capital Association).
- ➤ Industry and local technology associations.
- ➤ Professional advisors/mentors.
- ➤ Government sources (Federal/Provincial).
- ➤ Internet (Example: garage.com – Hewlett Packard's VC web site).

SELECTING A POTENTIAL INVESTOR – KEY ISSUES

This is a two-way process. It is essential to assess the potential investors' background and capabilities.

Investor selection check list:

- ➤ Character, reputation and credibility.
- ➤ Commitment and financial staying power (deep pockets). Will the investors be involved and have strong links to the next round of funding?
- ➤ Do they have the ability to bring other resources to the table, such as market and/or competitor knowledge. Do they understand prevailing industry and technology issues?
- ➤ What is their past track record? Have there been any problem investments?
- ➤ Compatibility. Is there a shared personal and business vision?
- ➤ References?

5. GETTING FACE-TO-FACE WITH POTENTIAL INVESTORS:

Some tips and tactics to achieve an effective live presentation:

- ➤ Practice the presentation beforehand – there are no second chances.
- ➤ Determine who from your team will be the presenter. This person should ideally be the company founder or CEO who is able to communicate his or her passion, commitment and staying power to the potential investor audience.

➤ Know your audience and tailor the message accordingly. Investors, corporate strategic partners or potential clients will require different presentations.

➤ Address the audience directly and establish eye contact. Do not read from previously prepared notes.

➤ Quickly arrive at the company's value proposition and uniqueness. It is critical that the audience understand and become excited at the opportunity facing them (reaching for their wallets).

➤ Seasoned investors and strategic partners will 'bet on the jockey, not the horse'. You need to demonstrate which key management people are now in place along with their strengths and experience. Investors or potential partners will not invest on the promise of hiring key personnel in the future.

➤ Product functionality does not have to be demonstrated at the presentation. Its effectiveness is a given and will be validated by a due-diligence process completed at a later date. Instead, focus on the market opportunity.

➤ Support the presentation with sales or marketing brochures which further illustrate the market potential.

➤ PowerPoint presentations are now the standard. While overheads are '1940's technology', they can be kept in reserve in case software or projector problems occur.

Some questions that you will be asked at the presentation:

➤ What is your background and track record?

➤ What is your financial commitment?

➤ Do you have a well-defined market niche that you can dominate (uniqueness)?

➤ Do you understand your customer and required sales channels?

➤ Detail your management team's experience and technical capabilities.

➤ How will the requested investment funds be used?

➤ What are your revenue and earnings growth assumptions?

➤ What is your competitive advantage? Who are your competitors? What are their relative strengths and weaknesses? Do you have any intellectual property barriers to entry?

➤ What steps have you taken to protect your intellectual property and ensure exclusivity with no strings attached? Were you working for someone else when you first developed the product or technology?

> What ROI will be achieved over the life of the investment? Is there a viable exit strategy?

> How will the proceeds of this investment influence your existing business strategy?

> What are your motivations – ego or wealth creation? (Ego implies a desire to 'stay at the helm' at all costs, even though the ship is sinking.)

> What are your weaknesses? This is a tough question that tests your willingness to disclose information. It is critical that you outline any challenges or obstacles frankly if you are to win the confidence of the potential investors.

OTHER ISSUES TO CONSIDER

> The initial introduction should take place through a respected intermediary (accountant, lawyer, commercial banker, local technology association.)

> Investors will complete an extensive due diligence review which will involve the following:

- ◆ checking your references
- ◆ reviewing legal agreements and bank authorities
- ◆ completing a facilities tour
- ◆ obtaining credit bureau reports
- ◆ analyzing historical financial statements
- ◆ reviewing financial projections and assumptions

> A due diligence information package will address the above points and should be prepared for the investors. They may elect to have some of their due diligence completed by an independent third party assessment report.

6. NEGOTIATING AND CLOSING THE DEAL

Key Points:

> The investor will issue a preliminary Term Sheet outlining the terms of the deal. This document needs to be carefully reviewed with your accountant and your lawyer.

> Further due diligence will take place by the investor prior to the completion of formal documentation and the shareholder agreement. This is an essential document which requires careful review with your legal advisors.

> ➤ A wide range of stakeholders have to be considered at this crucial stage so the closing process is invariably protracted (lots of lawyers).

> ➤ Time considerations: Raising capital is a time-consuming and often frustrating effort. No matter when you think it should be completed, it will take longer due to unforeseen delays, especially the preparation of legal documentation.

You can expedite this process by managing your lawyer's time by setting strict deadlines for documentation completion and execution. If lawyers on both sides are haggling over certain issues, convene a meeting with all the parties to hammer out and resolve the outstanding points.

7.   VALUATION ISSUES

In the previous chapter, company valuations based on 'going concern' criteria were discussed. With start-up companies, there have been no sales, stabilized earnings or cash flow that would allow you to perform a realistic valuation calculation.

An investor will be prepared to commit some new venture capital to a deal but will also want to attain a meaningful shareholding in the company. The following methodology describes how such an equity stake is derived.

The concept here is to project the valuation process 'into the future' by completing some simple future value calculations. (It should be noted that the same % ownership result can also be obtained by taking future earnings and completing a present value calculation.)

Assumptions

1. The enterprise requires $500,000 for new product and market development.

2. The investor, after assessing the venture's risk profile, determines that a 35% rate of return, compounded annually over five years, is required.

3. The company's financial projections estimate EBIT at $800,000 achieved at the end of Year Five. These projections have been carefully assessed and stress tested by the investor.

4. The investor's research indicates a current Industry price/earnings multiple in the 8x range.

Calculation

> The Future value of the company in Year Five based on the price/earnings multiple and forecast EBIT.

$$\$800,000 \times 8 \qquad = \$6.4 \text{ million}$$

> The future value of the investor's $500,000 investment, compounded (monthly) at 35% through to Year Five $= \$2.24 \text{ million}$

> Equity stake $= \dfrac{\$2.24}{\$6.40} \qquad\qquad = 35\%$

Therefore, the investor would negotiate a 35%+ stake in the company. The owner would retain 65%, having received a $500,000 equity injection to expedite product and market development.

If the company has a proven history of sales and positive earnings, potential investors would likely use a revenue multiple model (1 to 2 times annual revenues) based upon similar sale transactions observed in the specific industry sector.

USEFUL WEB SITES

www.strategis.ic.gc.ca	Industry Canada Strategis web site providing an excellent guide to business management resources including investment guidelines and success stories
www.businessfinance.com	Business capital search engine (USA)
www.wofund.com	GrowthWorks Ltd (Working Opportunity Fund) – venture capital reference site
www.ventureswest.com	Ventures West technology venture capital reference site

CHAPTER 10
MANAGING GROWTH

OVERVIEW

As companies in the tourism sector grow and mature, they make a transition from entrepreneurial management to professional management. Entrepreneurial management is characterized by centralized, often solo, decision making and a very informal style, control system and structure. Professional management involves more delegational decision making and use of formalized control systems. In this chapter, opportunities to grow the business will be examined.

It is important to note that growth requires further qualification. Is a company seeking growth in market share? Revenues? Margin? Earnings? Or a combination of all these?

The following areas will be covered:

1. Growth and development strategies.

2. Diversification – product or market growth?

1. GROWTH AND DEVELOPMENT STRATEGIES

Here are some questions that will help to assess a company's growth potential:

➤ Who are your customers now? Who will they be in the future?

➤ How do you reach your customers? What is your competitive advantage?

➤ Who is your competition now? Are new competitors anticipated in the future?

➤ Can you improve gross and net profit margins?

➤ Do you need to form new alliances? Can future strategic partners be identified?

Strategy comes from the Greek language and translates as 'the art of generalship'. The following four strategies are prevalent in most expanding and medium-sized companies. The key is to recognize which particular strategy provides your company with a competitive advantage.

A. DIFFERENTIATION

Companies can be 'different' in many ways by undertaking strategies that make them distinct from their competition. Some ways a company can set itself apart from the competition:

Customer service

> ➢ Customer Service.

> ➢ Friendliness.

> ➢ "Going the extra mile".

Product features

> ➢ Can new features or attributes be developed that will attract potential buyers?

> ➢ Can the product be improved by offering customized options?

Product packaging

> ➢ Consider how the product will be sold and what types of service programs can be offered.

Product quality

> ➢ Quality is often in the eye of the beholder (perception can be reality).

> ➢ The following checklist of quality characteristics might serve to differentiate your operations from the competition:

> > ◆ Durability and reliability.

> > ◆ Safety.

> > ◆ Consistent performance.

Service quality

> ➤ A similar list of quality characteristics can be developed for service industries:

  - ◆ Awareness of client needs and wants.

  - ◆ Dependability.

  - ◆ Sincerity.

  - ◆ Integrity.

  - ◆ Reputation of company as an employer.

  - ◆ Appropriate, "high touch" service levels for high-end service products.

B. Low-Cost Leadership

> ➤ Involves an intensive review of all company operations to identify and eliminate unnecessary costs.

> ➤ Is most effective in the tourism and hospitality industry where consumer buying decisions are price sensitive.

> ➤ Product simplicity can be developed by reducing cost inputs (materials, labor) which translates to a lower unit price. Such stripped-down products and services can be observed in most industry sectors. Examples:

  - ◆ Discount hotels: Days Inn, Holiday Inn Express.

  - ◆ Discount airlines: WestJet, SouthWest Airlines.

  - ◆ Discount brokerages: TD Waterhouse, Charles Schwab.

  - ◆ Warehouse stores: Canadian Tire, Costco.

> ➤ Implementation is the key. To assume a low-cost leadership role, the company's structure, reward systems and employee culture need to reflect the vision of a lean and effective organization.

C. Focus Strategies

Focus strategies that are aimed at either low-cost or differentiation opportunities involve concentrating on a smaller piece of the potential revenue pie. Examples:

> ➤ *Specialty products* that deliver non-standard items, i.e. adventure tourism, antique bathtubs.

> ➤ *Niches* are small, carefully defined market segments providing opportunities to exceed client expectations, i.e. small, upscale eco-tourism resorts.

> ➤ *Limited geographic territory.* Focus is on local or regional markets that have been overlooked by larger companies.

D. INTEGRATION

There are two types – Vertical and Horizontal.

1) Vertical: opportunities to expand arise within a company's own (vertical) industry sector.

   ♦ Backward integration – extends business activities 'back' toward raw materials and sources of supply.

   ♦ Forward integration – extends business activities 'forward' and closer to the company's marketplace, i.e. an airline offering complete vacation packages, or a food wholesaler establishing a retail outlet (taking care to ensure there is no direct competition with existing retail clients).

2) Horizontal: involves the assumption of increased control over competitors in a similar market. This usually translates to a merger or takeover which can be friendly (rescue or collaboration) or unfriendly (corporate raid).

2. DIVERSIFICATION – PRODUCT OR MARKET GROWTH?

Having reviewed various development strategies that can assist a company to grow with a tangible game plan, it is also instructive to assess growth opportunities from a product and market standpoint.

A Growth Directions Matrix (originally developed by Igor Ansoff) is an effective and graphic method that allows the summary of company product or market growth opportunities. This is illustrated by Figure 10-1 (opposite):

Figure 10 -1 Growth Directions Matrix

Product/Market Matrix

Markets

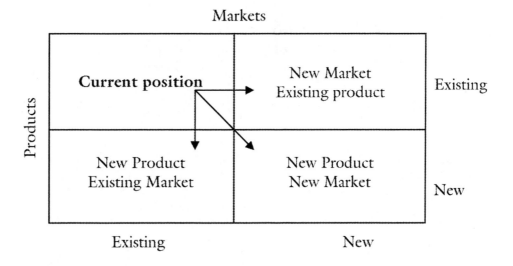

Consider the four options:

A. Existing Product and Market

♦ The status quo. Maintain steady growth doing everything a little better, every day.

♦ Growth is achieved by adopting a market penetration strategy, striving to increase market share for existing products or services.

B. New Market, Existing Product

♦ A market development strategy is implemented which involves finding a fresh market for existing products or services by:

    – expanding geographically (international expansion)

    – seeking new groups of customers

    – growing existing channel/distribution partnerships

C. New Product, Existing Market

♦ Involves the development of entirely new products (or devising additional features for existing products) that are targeted at existing customers.

D. New Product, New Markets

➤ This strategy involves setting off in a new direction and attempting to create new products in fresh markets. This is known as 'conglomerate diversification.'

➤ Becoming a 'new product, new market' pioneer entails significant risks. Before undertaking this strategy, a comprehensive review and assessment of company internal resources needs to take place.

CHAPTER 11
SOURCES OF DEBT FINANCING

OVERVIEW

In this chapter, sources of debt financing are reviewed. While there are no hard and fast rules, start-up companies are usually funded from equity sources (owner, seed capital, angels, etc.). Debt financing is often difficult to obtain.

Why is this?

The primary reason is cash flow. In order to obtain debt financing, a tourism based company typically has to be able to demonstrate that it can generate sustainable cash flow from its operations in order to service (pay interest) and repay any debt obligations. Many start-up companies struggle to become cash flow positive, and do not need a 'heavy backpack' of debt to burden their operations.

As a company matures and builds a solid track record of revenues, earnings and cash flow generation, a wide array of financing vehicles become available to them. Their next stage of growth can often be funded by both debt and additional equity streams like venture capital rounds.

This chapter also provides strategic tips that will assist you in negotiating mutually beneficial financing arrangements with your bank.

TYPES OF DEBT FINANCING

In this section, the following sources of financing are described:

1. Commercial banks.

2. Government initiatives.

3. Other types of debt financing.

1. COMMERCIAL BANKS

Commercial banks are the primary source of debt financing for small- and medium-sized companies. The different types of loans are detailed below:

A. OPERATING (REVOLVING) LINES OF CREDIT

Purpose:

 ➢ To finance short-term working capital needs (accounts receivable collection and inventory purchases).

Features:

 ➢ An authorized dollar limit is established based on a forecast of peak cash needs in any one month of the year.

 ➢ Borrowings are usually on demand, with a floating interest rate established at an agreed-upon percentage over the prevailing Prime rate (e.g. Prime + 1%).

 ➢ Operating borrowings are usually margined. You can only borrow up to a specified percentage of accounts receivable and inventories on your books as at a specific month end. e.g. 75% Accounts Receivable under 60 days, 50% Inventory at estimated cost.

 ➢ Security generally consists of a GSA (General Security Agreement) which provides the bank with a specific legal charge (claim) over your accounts receivable, inventory and (potentially) other company assets (known as a 'floating charge').

B. TERM LOANS

Purpose:

- ➤ Extended for equipment purchases with the term of the loan (three to seven years) matched to the expected life of the asset.

Features:

- ➤ Available on a floating or fixed-rate basis.

- ➤ Security will consist of a fixed, specific charge over the asset being acquired.

- ➤ Financing in 60% to 70% range is usually negotiable.

C. COMMERCIAL MORTGAGES

Purpose:

- ➤ To assist with the purchase/refinancing of commercial real estate.

Features:

- ➤ Usually available on a fixed-rate basis. Interest rates are locked in for one to seven year terms. Amortization periods are typically between 15 and 25 years depending on the quality and location of the real estate asset.

- ➤ Financing is available for up to 60% to 75% of current appraised value.

- ➤ Security consists of a first mortgage over the real estate asset along with an assignment of rents and fire insurance. Personal or corporate guarantees may also be required.

D. LETTERS OF CREDIT

Available for exporting or importing situations:

- ➤ Exporter wishes to sell goods or services but wants the assurance of payment before commencing production and delivery.

- ➤ Offshore importer wishes to purchase goods or services but does not wish to pay until shipping and title documents are received and are in good order.

E. BRIDGE LOANS

Interim financing is provided on a short-term basis to cover project costs pending inflow of sales proceeds or long-term financing.

Example: A real estate construction project (townhouses) is to be built. Construction and interest costs will be financed by the bank pending sale of the townhouse units.

F. CREDIT CARDS

Expense and purchasing cards for the business.

G. PERSONAL LOANS

Available to the company owner to raise additional funds and then inject into the company by way of a shareholder loan.

2. GOVERNMENT INITIATIVES

A. SMALL BUSINESS LOAN ASSISTANCE

Features:

- ➢ SBLA loans are available from banks for amounts of up to $250,000.
- ➢ 85% of the value of the loan is guaranteed by the federal government.
- ➢ Loan proceeds are used for the acquisition of land, buildings, and machinery. (Note: this program does not cover inventory financing.)
- ➢ Fixed or floating rates (Prime + 3% including a loan loss reserve premium).
- ➢ 2% fee loan registration fee.
- ➢ Terms up to 10 years.

B. IRAP (INDUSTRIAL RESEARCH ASSOCIATION PROGRAMS)

Part of the National Research Council. IRAP programs provide financial assistance (on a match-funding basis) to technology companies for R&D and new technology assessments.

C. SR & ED

Scientific Research and Experimental Development tax rebates are available to qualifying technology companies.

D. PEMD

Program for Experimental Market Development. Financial assistance is provided to companies to attend international trade shows.

3. OTHER TYPES OF DEBT FINANCING

A. LEASING

- ➤ Available from banks, equipment manufacturers and lease financing companies for business equipment and larger ticket items.
- ➤ Lease terms typically run from 36 to 60 months and cover 100% cost of the asset being leased.

Benefits:

- ➤ Preserves working capital (cash) for expansion purposes.
- ➤ Leaves operating credit lines available for non-fixed asset financing needs.
- ➤ Provides a hedge against equipment obsolescence.

Note: It is important to obtain professional advice from your accountant to ensure that there are favourable tax consequences arising from leasing versus borrowing to purchase.

Figure 11-1 (next page) summarizes the buying versus leasing decision and the resultant ownership relationships.

Figure 11-1 Buy or Lease

BUY OR LEASE?

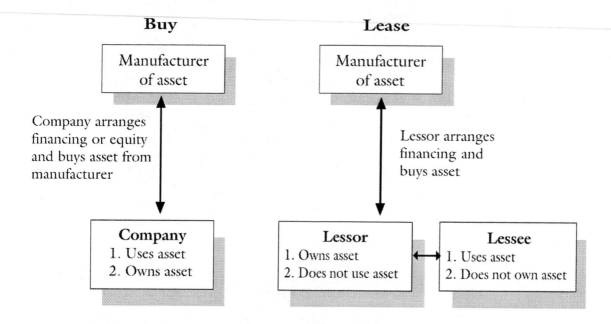

B. FLOOR PLAN FINANCING

Loans provided by manufacturers which allow retailers or distributors to acquire product (inventory) and make it available for sale. The floor loan is repaid from the product sales proceeds.

C. MEZZANINE FINANCING

Also known as a subordinated debt ('sub debt'). This is a form of financing that falls between traditional debt and equity on the balance sheet.

Features:

> Relatively high interest rates (12% to 15%) provide the mezzanine lender with a reasonable return relative to the risk profile of the company.

Plus

> An equity component, usually warrants, that enables the lender to acquire future equity (15% to 25%) of the company.

Benefits:

- ➤ Targeted at rapid growth companies that need supplemental funding over and above traditional sources of debt and equity.

- ➤ Sub debt lenders look primarily at the company's cash flow and 'enterprise value' for payment and return on equity as opposed to more traditional lenders who derive comfort from the book value of assets which have been pledged as collateral.

- ➤ Cheaper than pure equity investments and more flexible than conventional debt.

- ➤ Board seats are not usually required.

- ➤ Typical underwriting criteria:

- ➤ Strong management in place with a significant ownership stake in the business.

- ➤ The company is experiencing strong revenue growth (minimum 20% per year).

- ➤ Cash flow positive (EBITDA).

- ➤ Other sophisticated investors (venture capital firms) and lenders (banks) are also participating.

- ➤ A defined exit strategy is in place (i.e. an Initial Public Offering (IPO), re-financing, or sale of the company).

D. RESTRUCTURING LOAN PAYMENTS

- ➤ 'Interest only' through slow cash flow periods.

- ➤ Balloon payments at the end of a loan term, thereby lowering prior principal monthly payments.

- ➤ Seasonal 'lump sum' principal payments.

E. BOOTSTRAP FINANCING

Bootstrap financing arises when a venture is launched with modest personal funds and is then 'bootstrapped' up the growth curve by implementing creative survival strategies. Close attention to cash flow and cash resources is a key feature of this process.

Some strategies from the world of bootstrap finance:

Factoring

> ➤ A company (factor) purchases your accounts receivable, advancing 70% to 90% of a specific invoice amount.

> ➤ Servicing fees (2% value of the receivable) are charged along with an interest rate (Prime + 3% plus) on funds advanced prior to the collection of the invoice.

> ➤ This can be an alternative source of financing for companies that do not yet qualify for operating credit lines.

> ➤ No additional liabilities are added to the Balance Sheet (existing accounts receivable are merely discounted by the factoring company).

> ➤ The accelerated receipt of cash can relieve seasonal cash flow pressures and allow companies to take advantage of trade discounts from suppliers and/or special product purchase opportunities.

Customer Credit

> ➤ It may be possible to negotiate with your clients to provide advance payments in the early stages of a particular project.

Supplier Credit

> ➤ Trade credit terms can be negotiated with suppliers, often with long lead times to allow for seasonal impacts on the cash flow cycle (another cash driver strategy).

Landlord Credit

> ➤ Financial assistance from your landlord (assuming that the premises are rented) may be available to complete additional leasehold improvements. Temporary deferral of monthly rent during a tight cash flow period may also be negotiable.

Other "bootstrap" initiatives to consider

> ➤ Expand slowly and carefully. While 'first mover advantage' may be lost, the slow and steady approach to expansion means less pressure on limited working capital resources.

- Minimize unnecessary capital expenditures.

- Have employees accept stock options or profit sharing in lieu of industry standard wages until the business becomes more established.

- With custom orders, negotiate a 30% - 60% - 10% payment structure from customers: 30% up front, 60% upon delivery and a 10% holdback to cover performance issues.

- Try to acquire a 'lighthouse client': a well-known and credible industry leader who will serve as an attractive reference to other potential clients, corporate strategic partners and investors.

DEALING WITH BANKS

In this section, the following issues are reviewed:

1. How to build a strong relationship with your bank

2. The loan approval process – some key issues

3. How bankers 'risk assess' your company

4. A sample financing commitment letter

1. HOW TO BUILD A STRONG RELATIONSHIP WITH YOUR BANKER – FIVE KEY STEPS

LOCATE THE RIGHT BANKER

If you are seeking a new bank, remember that the key to an enduring relationship will be the individual commercial banker. Questions to ask:

- What are your qualifications and length of commercial lending experience?

- Do you have a team approach to commercial banking relationships? Who provides ongoing support to you and to whom do you report?

- Provide an overview of your commercial loan portfolio. Which industries do you specialize in and where have you had the most success?

- How important is commercial banking and the tourism sector to your bank?

DEMONSTRATE CREDIBILITY AND RELIABILITY

- ➤ Through business plan presentations, demonstrate your intimate knowledge of company operations, major competitors and industry opportunities and threats.

- ➤ Under promise and over deliver.

- ➤ Provide credible, accurate and timely financial information as part of your monthly reporting and annual review process.

- ➤ Anticipate financing needs early (i.e. temporary bulges, new capital financing needs).

- ➤ Invite your banker to your place of business and provide a tour and an introduction to key personnel.

BUILD A TEAM OF PROFESSIONAL ADVISORS

- ➤ Your banker will want to know who provides you with accounting, legal, and strategic advice. He/she will likely know these professionals personally.

- ➤ Do not hesitate to involve your accountant in any complex or difficult loan negotiations.

COMMUNICATE

- ➤ Keep your banker informed regarding any issues (positive or negative) that might impact your business operations or industry segment.

- ➤ Report bad news or deteriorating trends early, along with a plan of action to deal with them. Avoid providing your bank with unpleasant surprises.

- ➤ Let the bank know whether or not they are meeting your expectations. Get issues out on the table quickly.

SEEK OUT OTHER RESOURCES

Your bank is far more than a place to borrow money. Other areas where support can be provided include:

- ➤ Cash management services:
    - ◆ Allow the monitoring of account activities and transfer of funds via the Internet.

- ◆ B2B services: electronic portals that allow you to expand supplier/ client contacts.

- ◆ Pay interest income on commercial deposit balances.

➤ Trade finance: export/import assistance.

➤ Foreign exchange: currency conversions and hedging strategies.

➤ Interest rate hedging: for larger clients, strategies are available that swap floating for fixed interest rates, and establish caps/floors to minimize future interest rate fluctuations.

Your banker also runs a business within a business with a portfolio of commercial clients that forms part of the bank's overall loan and deposit portfolio. Like any successful business, commercial bankers have to grow their client base, provide outstanding customer service, and deliver profitable returns to their shareholders.

2. THE LOAN APPLICATION PROCESS

KEY ISSUES:

Before you commence an application for a new or increased commercial loan, consider the simple acronym WARS:

➤ Why do you need the financing?

➤ Amount: will it be sufficient?

➤ Repayment: how do you plan to repay the loan and over what period of time?

➤ Security: what collateral are you prepared to offer?

A short written presentation should be completed that outlines your financing requirement along with supporting company financial statements and/or projections and a current personal financial statement. Even if personal guarantees are not required, the depth of pockets of company principals will often be a key component of the bank's risk assessment process.

SPECIFIC GUIDELINES

Operating Line – New or expanded facility

- ➢ Define purpose: financing receivables, working capital requirements, etc.

- ➢ Indicate dollar amount and demonstrate need with monthly cash flow projections.

- ➢ Margin conditions: 75% eligible receivables, 50% cost inventory.

- ➢ Work in progress (WIP) margin may be feasible.

- ➢ Provide receivable/payable listings along with inventory breakdowns.

- ➢ Interest rate (usually Prime + 1% or lower).

- ➢ Monthly loan administration fees (often negotiable).

Term Loan/Mortgage -New or increased

- ➢ Indicate purpose and dollar amount required.

- ➢ Detail the repayment term, and amortization desired. Amortization should match the economic life of the asset that is being financed.

- ➢ Cash flow coverage – should be a minimum of 1.25x.

- ➢ Property and equipment appraisals should be current and prepared by credible professionals.

- ➢ Provide insurance details along with an environmental assessment and indemnity.

- ➢ Interest rate (fixed or floating): how does the offered rate compare to the other lenders?

- ➢ Application fees (sometimes negotiable).

COLLATERAL

- ➢ GSA (General Security Agreement).

- ➢ Section 427 Bank Act (for inventory financing).

- ➢ Collateral mortgage/assignment of rents (for commercial properties).

- ➢ Chattel Mortgage (for equipment loans).

OTHER COLLATERAL ISSUES

➤ Personal guarantees will often be required, especially if the company does not have a track record of revenue/earnings growth and a strong balance sheet.

> The bank will usually need a second way out if mishaps or serious problems occur. The primary way out is the company's ongoing ability to generate sustainable cash flow, backed up by the assets (accounts receivable, inventory, property) that fuel the cash generation.

> If this process becomes seriously impaired, then recourse to other avenues of repayment (personal assets and resources) becomes an important second line of defense to a lender.

➤ Subrogations: These are encountered when shareholder loans are postponed to the bank's security interest. In effect, these equity funds may not be withdrawn or reduced without bank approval. Subrogated shareholder loans are often included in equity calculations for leverage test covenants.

➤ Assignment of life and/or disability insurance: The bank will often request assignment of key-person life and/or disability insurance, especially if succession plans are not clearly defined.

FINANCIAL TEST COVENANTS

➤ These are often included in bank term sheets and offers of credit. They can best be described as financial benchmarks that need to be met on an annual basis, evidenced by the client's (audited or review engagement) financial statements.

➤ Some examples of financial benchmarks include:

> Working capital ratio – minimum 2:1.
> Debt to equity ratio – maximum 1.5:1.
> Debt service coverage – minimum 1.25x.

➤ Each test covenant will have the relevant financial ratio calculation clearly defined.

MONITORING REQUIREMENTS

➤ Operating lines of credit will involve prompt provision of monthly accounts receivable, accounts payable, and inventory listings. These are often accompanied by interim monthly or quarterly in-house financial statements so that ongoing performance can be measured against the prior year and budget (forecast).

3. BANK RISK ASSESSMENT

Once a loan proposal has been presented to the commercial banker, the internal loan application commences. This is a complex process with internal negotiation often taking place between the front-line bankers and the bank's credit department. A key ingredient of a company's successful loan approval is the completion of a detailed risk assessment by the front-line bankers for the credit department review.

Tourism company owners can greatly enhance this process by providing a comprehensive information package to their banker. It is important that company owners gain a greater understanding of this risk assessment process. It is their company going under the microscope!

A bank's risk assessment process can be segmented into the following key areas, each with a check-list of questions and issues to consider:

- Company strategy
- Market potential
- Infrastructure and operations
- Financial performance
- Management capability

COMPANY STRATEGY

- Is the company's competitive strategy based on:

    Cost/price leadership?

    Differentiation of products or services?

    . Focus on distinctive market segments?

- Which of the following generic corporate strategies have been implemented?

    Diversification

    Integration (Vertical or Horizontal)

    Licensing

    Outsourcing

    Joint ventures or corporate alliances

➤ What are the company's sustainable competitive advantages?

➤ What are the key success factors necessary to prosper in the particular industry segment?

MARKET POTENTIAL

➤ What is the market size? Is there an over reliance on a few large clients or is there a well-spread, balanced clientele?

➤ Is there reliance on a single or a few distributors?

➤ How stable is market demand?

➤ Assess the market acceptance of the company's products or services.

➤ How vulnerable is the company to competition?

➤ What are the current selling terms? Cash required on delivery or receivable terms?

INFRASTRUCTURE AND OPERATIONS

➤ Consider environmental controls and regulations (present and proposed).

➤ Review fixed assets: location, characteristics, condition and adequacy. Are the premises owned or leased? Is adequate insurance in place?

➤ If applicable, what is the length of the manufacturing cycle and how controllable are manufacturing costs?

➤ Assess the price stability and availability of raw materials and other inputs.

➤ Review inventory: Mix, location, characteristics, condition and the ability to liquidate?

➤ Assess the adequacy, stability and quality of labour. Is the workforce unionized or is there potential for union involvement?

FINANCIAL PERFORMANCE

➤ How reliable and current is financial information? Have year-end financial statements been prepared by an accredited accounting firm?

➤ Are there any 'off balance sheet' issues to consider? Is there a large appraisal surplus in company owned land and buildings?

➤ Assess working capital adequacy and cash driver performance. Measure liquidity by inventory turnover, accounts payable settlement, and accounts receivable collection ratios.

➤ What is the relationship between debt and equity? What are the historical trends?

➤ Is there adequate equity to support expanding sales? Look for symptoms of over-trading (insufficient working capital base to support rapidly growing sales). Is there adequate cash flow to finance growth?

➤ What is the trend for revenues (volume and mix)?

➤ Assess revenue and gross margin performance and trends. Review control of expenses and determine the extent of fixed overhead?

➤ Are there any foreign exchange risks (export or import)?

➤ How adequate is the company's financial planning and related controls? Are regular (monthly, quarterly) financial statements completed on an in-house basis contrasting prior year, current year and budget performance?

MANAGEMENT CAPABILITY

➤ Examine the stability of owner's control: Are share holdings held on an amicable basis or is there potential for conflict? Is there a buy-sell agreement (along with an appropriate shot-gun clause) in place between the two controlling entities?

➤ Do the owners have the ability to inject funds from sources outside the company?

➤ Do the company owners have 'hands on skills' to manage daily operations?

➤ Are there any related company borrowing requirements? What is their reliance upon the borrower, or the borrower's reliance upon them? A corporate family tree is always helpful in describing more complex business structures.

➤ Are aggressive expansion plans being contemplated? Have such expansion plans been carefully conceived – are they in line with company working capital, equity base and earnings capacity?

➤ Continuity and succession: Is there a clearly defined chain of command along with identified personnel who can step into the shoes of existing management?

4. EXTRACTS FROM A TYPICAL BANK COMMITMENT LETTER:

BORROWER:
Johnston Air Tours

FACILITY:
Operating Loan Facility in the amount of $150,000, subject to the terms and conditions as outlined below.

RATE:
Bank Prime Rate plus one percent per annum (Prime+1%) floating, accrued from day to day, calculated and payable monthly, in arrears, based on a calendar year.

PRIME RATE:
'Prime Rate' means the floating annual rate of interest established from time to time by the bank as the reference rate it will use to determine rates of interest on Canadian dollar loans, to borrowers in Canada.

MARGIN CONDITIONS:
Availability of the operating credit is subject to a maximum of:

75% of the bank's valuation of assigned accounts receivable after deducting those 61 days or more past due, accounts in dispute, inter company accounts, contra accounts and the value of any prior ranking claims.

Plus:

50% of the bank's valuation at cost, of assigned inventory which is free and clear, excluding work in process, consignment inventory or inventory subject to any prior charge or claim. The maximum margin value of inventory will be $50,000.

MARGIN REPORTING:
Within twenty-one (21) days after the last calendar day of each month the following information should be delivered to the bank:

➤ A certified aged list of outstanding accounts receivable identifying accounts in dispute, inter company accounts, contra accounts and the value of any prior ranking claims.

➤ A certified valuation of inventory excluding any items held on a consignment basis, and identifying all inventory subject to prior charges or claims in favour of other creditors.

➤ An aged list of outstanding accounts payable.

GENERAL CONDITIONS:

- Monthly company prepared Financial Statements (Balance Sheet and Income Statement) are to be provided within 30 days of month end.

- Annual company prepared Financial Statements (Review Engagement) are to be provided within 120 days of fiscal year end.

- A signed personal financial statement of Jim Johnston to be provided concurrently with annual financial statements.

SECURITY:

Prior to any funds being advanced to the borrower by the bank, the following security documents should be executed, registered and delivered in a form and content satisfactory to the Bank.

- Appropriate documentation evidencing corporate authority.

- Registered General Assignment of Book Debts.

- Assignment of Inventory via Section 427 of the Bank Act.

- Registered General Security Agreement providing the bank with a first charge over all assets.

- Assignment of All Perils Insurance for Equipment and Inventory, with first loss payable to the bank.

- An unlimited personal guarantee from Jim and Ann Johnston.

- Subrogation via promissory note of shareholder loans total $96,000.

FINANCIAL COVENANTS:

- Capital expenditures are not to exceed $200,000 in any fiscal year without prior bank written approval.

- Total debt to equity ratio will not exceed 2:1 at any time. Equity is defined as retained earnings, subrogated shareholder loans, and share capital.

- Working capital ratio minimum 1.25:1 is to be maintained.

EXPENSES:

The borrower will be responsible for the following:

- ➤ All legal and other professional fees for searching, preparing, execution and registration of all loan and security documentation.

- ➤ All other costs and out-of-pocket expenses incurred by the bank in connection with the establishment and administration of the facilities and the obtaining of applicable security.

Please signify your acceptance of these terms by signing and returning the attached copy of this commitment letter.

USEFUL WEB SITES

www.cba.ca   Canadian Bankers Association – useful sections on resolving problems with your bank and business financing sources

www.ibm.com/financing   IBM asset financing solutions

CHAPTER 12
SURVIVAL STRATEGIES

OVERVIEW

Studies indicate that four out of five start-up companies cease to exist after five years. This chapter is written on the premise that the more you know about 'the dark side of the moon', the less chance there will be that your tourism company will become another statistic. The chapter is divided into the following sections:

1. Causes of business failures

2. External warning signals

3. Internal warning signals

4. Turnaround strategies and options

1. CAUSES OF BUSINESS FAILURES

The authors have observed many successful companies prosper and expand. We have also seen companies 'come off the rails', sometimes permanently. Business failures can often be attributed to the following causes:

- Managerial or key employee problems.

- Product or market difficulties.

- Financial weakness.

Some examples of poor management decisions and unwisely executed strategies that have led to corporate oblivion follow:

- ➤ Embarking on an ambitious expansion project with too much debt and not enough equity.

- ➤ Venturing into new (offshore) markets without sufficient market research.

- ➤ Lack of 'hands-on' management, coupled with a lack of inclination to jump in and fix potentially costly operational problems.

- ➤ Shareholder disputes aggravated by an absence of buy/sell agreements and shotgun clauses.

- ➤ "Big Box" and cross-border retailer incursions (Home Depot, Costco etc.) Similarly, the appearance of large, name-brand franchises that overshadow smaller, independent operators.

- ➤ Significant receivables with protracted payment terms that result in stifled cash flow.

- ➤ Attempting an industry 'consolidation' play without the financial and operational resources to digest an acquisition target.

- ➤ Complex management and information systems installed at great cost that lead to greater disruption and little tangible benefit.

- ➤ Business failure of a supplier who provided critical components or equipment for a new contract.

2. EXTERNAL WARNING SIGNALS

- ➤ Adverse legal, political and regulatory changes.

- ➤ Cultural and social changes that alter consumer preferences or product awareness. (For example, the effect of September 11th on people's willingness to travel.)

- ➤ Failure to anticipate an accelerating pace of technological change.

- ➤ Weakening of general economic conditions evidenced by inflationary trends, budget deficits, higher government taxes and reduced consumer spending.

- ➤ Increasing interest rates allied with tightening bank credit availability and stricter lending guidelines.

➤ Industry issues:

  ◆ Intensified competition overcoming historic barriers to entry.

  ◆ Emergence of substitute products.

  ◆ Increasing supplier and buyer power.

3. INTERNAL WARNING SIGNALS

A. FINANCIAL

➤ Tightened liquidity, evidenced by:

  ◆ Delays in collecting accounts receivable, along with increases in bad debt expense.

  ◆ Difficulties in meeting accounts payable obligations.

  ◆ Bank overdrafts and locked-in operating credits.

  ◆ Lack of an understanding of bank margin conditions.

➤ Under-capitalization:

  ◆ Reliance on debt to finance operating losses.

  ◆ Weakened retained earnings due to historical operating losses that have become 'acceptable'.

  ◆ Inability to attract additional capital. Existing shareholders are 'tapped out' and do not have deep pockets.

➤ Lack of financial information:

  ◆ Absence of current monthly or quarterly financial statements.

  ◆ Poor or non-existent cash flow monitoring and analysis.

  ◆ Weak financial information control systems that have failed to keep pace with the company's growth and increasingly complex operations.

➤ Declining revenues, gross profit margins and earnings.

➤ Over-trading trends, where working capital resources are insufficient to fund aggressive revenue growth.

➤ Unexpected increases in fixed costs.

➤ Increased inventory levels without commensurate revenue increases.

➤ Dealing with too many banks and long-term lenders.

B. PRODUCTS AND MARKETS

➤ Inadequate current market research and failure to 'listen to the market place'.

➤ High concentration of sales to one, or a small handful, of customers.

➤ Increasing failure to meet product sales and market penetration targets.

➤ Timing difficulties in launching new products.

➤ Overly complex distribution and selling strategies.

➤ Lack of ongoing product and service innovation.

C. MANAGEMENT AND KEY EMPLOYEES

➤ Lack of clear business vision and guidance from key professional advisors and board members.

➤ High turnover rates among key employees.

➤ Delayed presentation of management and financial reports.

➤ Overly complex corporate structure with numerous subsidiaries and involved inter-company transactions.

➤ Obsession with tax-avoidance strategies.

➤ Employees with more than one boss or supervisor (matrix organizational structure).

➤ Delegation without control or feedback.

➤ Senior management abuse of benefits and compensation plans.

➤ Personal problems (divorce, family succession issues and disputes).

➤ Fraudulent activities, which could include the following:

♦ Unexplained inventory shrinkage
♦ Negligent financial reporting
♦ Diversion of funds

4. TURNAROUND STRATEGIES AND OPTIONS

In general, a turnaround strategy can be implemented by adopting the following process (with appropriate time lines):

1. Evaluation and creation of a recovery plan (from one to three months).

2. Implementation (three to six months).

3. Stabilization of the business and return to growth (six months to a year).

It is crucial to commence the turnaround strategy on an urgent basis and have the first step take place as quickly as possible. The remaining implementation and stabilization steps will take more time. Companies are not turned around overnight; however, time is still a key consideration.

Note: Before beginning the turnaround process, solvency and viability need to be considered.

SOLVENCY

In most cases, a company is said to be solvent if it is able to meet its obligations as they become due, and the net realization value of its assets will cover its liabilities.

VIABILITY

A viable company is one that is able to carry on profitable operations now and into the medium term. If the company is not viable, it is not worth expending valuable resources in an attempt to save it.

In assessing the viability of a distressed business, some key questions must be considered:

➤ Is there a sufficient depth of market (awareness) for the company products or services?

➤ Is there an effective sales force in place to market the product or service?

➤ Are reasonable gross margins being obtained?

If the company is neither solvent nor viable, formal liquidation and wind-down will take place through receivership or bankruptcy proceedings. This process is complex, expensive and beyond the intention and scope of this book. If a company is solvent and appears reasonably viable, the following steps will have to take place:

A. Evaluation of each functional area.

B. Implementation of financial and operational turnaround strategies.

A. THE EVALUATION PROCESS

FINANCIAL RESOURCES:

- ➤ Check for excessively high accounts receivable and inventories. Can they be collected or reduced to generate cash?

- ➤ Assess the potential for sale and lease-back of fixed assets. This can often be another source of cash generation.

MARKETING RESOURCES:

- ➤ Analyze revenue and profitability trends by market segment.

- ➤ Verify product 'acceptance' in the marketplace (quality and customer need issues). How effective is after-sales service?

- ➤ Check gross profit margin performance by major product lines.

OPERATIONAL RESOURCES:

- ➤ If the business is a manufacturing operation, establish the percentage of production capacity that is currently used.

- ➤ Check for obsolete production equipment.

- ➤ Identify any procurement problems.

HUMAN RESOURCES:

- ➢ Assess employee turnover and wage/salary costs relative to industry standards.

- ➢ Question senior management about the cause of the present downturn and how they would resolve it. What capability and commitment do they have to turn the company around?

- ➢ Can the company's organizational structure be simplified?

B. THE IMPLEMENTATION PROCESS

Once the evaluation process has been completed, the following turnaround strategies can be considered for implementation:

FINANCIAL

- ➢ Increase revenues and market penetration through cost-effective advertising and lower prices.

- ➢ Reduce surplus and redundant assets by selective sell-off.

- ➢ Restructure debt by extending amortization, negotiating interest and/or principal holidays. In rare cases, debt forgiveness (usually with unsecured creditors) can be negotiated.

- ➢ Arrange equity injections through existing shareholders, possibly employees, outside investors, or government sources.

- ➢ Convince clients to provide up-front cash payments to pay for raw materials and supplies.

OPERATIONAL

- ➢ Restructure the company's organization to flatten reporting relationships and to re-align operations around a reduced number of product lines and/or market segments.

- ➢ Merge with, or be acquired by, a compatible company. Such a step can provide financial, operational and technical support to an ailing company.

- ➢ Initiate selective but effective cost-cutting measures. These could include pay concessions by employees (hopefully short-term pain for longer-term gain) or restructuring from salary to commission payment systems.

SUMMARY

With any of the aforementioned turnaround strategies, one critical need emerges: everyone – management, employees, landlord, trade creditors, clients, banks, shareholders, directors – needs to pull together in a concerted effort to drive the turnaround forward.

USEFUL WEB SITES

www.smartbiz.com   Small business survival tips

SECTION 4

STRATEGIC PLANNING

CHAPTER 13
BUSINESS AND STRATEGIC PLANS

OVERVIEW

The business planning process is essential to the success of all enterprises. Some guidelines and tips in the crafting of effective business and strategic plans are provided in this chapter.

While there are numerous templates and guides for business plan completion, developing a comprehensive plan is difficult due to the multitude of purposes such plans encounter. To simplify (and demystify) the process, the following audiences have been segmented:

> External (investors, bankers, other lenders)
>
> *and*
>
> Internal (senior management, employees, Boards of Directors or Advisors)

Each audience will receive a different set of plans which are detailed in the following sections:

External Audiences

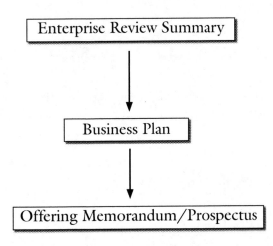

Internal Audiences

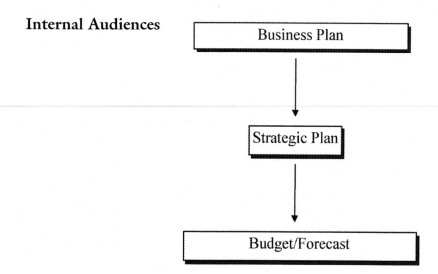

The Business Plan is common to both audiences; however, External Audiences will typically receive an initial overview of an investment or banking opportunity by way of a short and simple "Enterprise Review Summary" (ERS).

Following completion of the Business Plan, if an investment opportunity is being pursued, a public offering and/or private placement process may be initiated via another set of documents, the Offering Memorandum and/or Prospectus.

Internal Audiences will also have the opportunity to review the Business Plan, which acts as a foundation document. It is then followed by a Strategic Plan, along with a detailed budget and forecast.

After reviewing the key features of these various planning documents, business plan features that either succeed or detract are examined. Several tips on the effective packaging and presentation of Business Plans are also presented.

1. EXTERNAL AUDIENCES

While clients and suppliers sometimes comprise the external audience, the focus on this presentation will be to investors and/or lenders, because raising external funding remains a key challenge for many start-up and growing companies.

THE ENTERPRISE REVIEW SUMMARY

The ERS is a simple two- or three-page, plain language document describing how an investor will make money from a product, service, or process generated by a company. If financing is required, the form of security and repayment will be described.

In essence, the ERS is an initial "hook", and is often fine-tuned to form the executive summary in a formal Business Plan. The primary components of the ERS are:

- The opportunity, for either the investor or lender
- The company and key management
- Products or Services
- Markets
- Financial performance and projections
- Pay-back: Investors – return on investment and exit point
- Lenders – debt retirement and time frame

Each of these headings will be followed by a maximum of two to three paragraphs. The pay-back section that is addressed to lenders would only be completed if the company was in a positive cash flow position.

THE BUSINESS PLAN

In this section, the key components of a Business Plan are presented, along with some supplementary issues to consider within each section. The Business Plan structure can be summarized as follows:

- The executive summary
- Company and/or project description
- Marketing plan
- Production and operations plan
- Financing plan
- Management plan
- Appendices

EXECUTIVE SUMMARY

A one- to three-page overview of the complete business plan. It is essential to have this section written after the other sections are completed. A ERS can be fine-tuned to meet this requirement.

COMPANY/PROJECT DESCRIPTION

Explains the type of company and provides a history, if already in existence. It also describes the proposed form of organization, including the company's objectives. A more detailed description of products or services is provided, together with features that provide a competitive advantage. Intellectual property issues are also addressed.

ISSUES TO CONSIDER:

- ♦ Is the company's overall strategy consistent with prevailing industry opportunities and threats?

- ♦ Are the company's objectives consistent with its resources – financial, marketing, operations, technology, etc.?

MARKETING PLAN

This section details the company's customers and what type of competition will be encountered. Key features that should be included are:

- ➤ Identification of market segments.

- ➤ Analysis of target markets and profile of target customers.

- ➤ Methods to identify and attract customers.

- ➤ Selling approaches.

- ➤ Type of sales force and distribution channels.

- ➤ Tactics – the 4 P's – Price, Product, Place, Promotion.

ISSUES TO CONSIDER:

- ♦ Is there a high dependence on a limited number of clients?

- ♦ Is there limited control of pricing and distribution channels?

- ♦ Has a detailed competition assessment been completed?

PRODUCTION/OPERATIONS PLAN

This segment describes the type of manufacturing or operating systems that will be used.

Key features include:

- ➢ Operating and manufacturing methods.
- ➢ Description of operating facilities.
- ➢ Quality control procedures.
- ➢ Sources of supply and purchasing (procurement) methods.

ISSUES TO CONSIDER:

- ◆ Does the company have an appropriate location in relation to clients, suppliers, employees, and access to technology resources?
- ◆ Is there a dependence on a few key suppliers?
- ◆ Is there adequate capacity in relation to projected sales?
- ◆ Are there any potential environmental hazards?

FINANCIAL PLAN

This section specifies the financial needs of the company, together with contemplated sources of funding, and will include:

- ➢ Historical financial statements (for the last three to five years), including projected Balance Sheets, Income Statements, and Cash Flow statements. These should be provided on a monthly basis for the first year, and quarterly thereafter.
- ➢ A breakeven analysis together with an indication of funding sources and allocation of proceeds.

ISSUES TO CONSIDER:

- ◆ Does the forecasted EBT reveal steady growth in line with present industry norms?
- ◆ Will a breakeven point be reached within two years, if it is a start up operation?
- ◆ Is the forecasted ROI less than 20%? This would be considered weak from an investor's point of view.

- Does the forecasted EBITDA provide sufficient debt service coverage (from a lender's standpoint)?

- Do the projected balance sheets reveal too much leverage (high debt to equity ratio)?

MANAGEMENT PLAN

This section identifies the key players, including the management team, directors, and any investors already in place. The management team's qualifications are described. Outside resource people are also identified, along with their qualifications.

ISSUES TO CONSIDER:

- Do senior managers have a shareholding interest in the company?

- Are the necessary marketing, operational, and financial skills in place or attainable in the near term?

OFFERING MEMORANDUM/PROSPECTUS

When companies decide to raise additional equity, through either an initial public offering (IPO) or private placement, various regulatory ERSies will require the publication of an Offering Memorandum or Prospectus. This documentation details the investment opportunity to potential investors, together with a comprehensive disclosure of risk factors. Detailed capital and share structure information is also provided.

A more comprehensive review of the IPO and private placement process is not the intention of this book. Additional details can be obtained from local brokerage houses or venture capital firms.

2. INTERNAL AUDIENCES

BUSINESS PLAN

Use the same format as established for external audiences.

STRATEGIC PLAN

The strategic plan is an internal document and contains the following sections:

1. Strategic direction and vision.
2. External and internal size-up.
3. Key findings and tactics.
4. Action plans and milestones.

1. STRATEGIC DIRECTION AND VISION

Addresses the following areas:

- Vision Statement – What we want to be.
- Mission Statement – What we do.
- Goal identification (i.e., revenue growth, customer satisfaction, technical excellence).
- Business description – product or service road maps.
- Key markets – sustainable advantage evaluation.
- Objectives – SMART (specific, measurable, achievable, realistic, time framed).

2. EXTERNAL AND INTERNAL SIZE-UP

External:

- PEST Analysis.
- Industry analysis, including a review of opportunities and threats.

Internal:

- ➢ Finance
- ➢ Marketing
- ➢ Operations
- ➢ Human Resources
- ➢ Technology

An evaluation of strengths and weaknesses will take place for each segment.

3. KEY FINDINGS AND TACTICS

These are applied to the various finance, marketing, operations, human resources, and technology sectors.

4. ACTION PLANS AND MILESTONES

These are allocated to all the aforementioned categories, indicating who will do what, when and how. The relative cost of these initiatives should also be determined.

BUDGET AND FORECAST

The budget is an internal document containing the balance sheet (quarterly), income statement and cash flow (monthly), together with capital expenditure forecasts and cost centre breakdowns by department.

The forecast is a monthly projection detailing key financial performance areas such as bookings, revenue, inventory, and cash flow.

In assessing the budget and forecast documents, two key steps need to be followed:

1) ESTABLISH SPECIFIC OBJECTIVES

Example:

- ➢ Increase revenues by 15% on an annual basis.
- ➢ Maintain gross profit margins at 45%.

These objectives will usually evolve from the key findings and tactics in the finance section of the internal size-up.

2) SET UP TRACKING AND CONTROL SYSTEMS

Example:

- Quarterly review: Balance sheet, capital expenditures.

- Monthly review: Profit and loss statement, cash flow statement, etc.

SEVEN WAYS TO CREATE AN EFFECTIVE BUSINESS PLAN

1. FOCUS ON THE MARKET

- Strive to be market driven (meeting customer needs), rather than technology driven. The potential of the marketplace and resulting revenue/earnings is far more important than a product's technical features.

- Demonstrate the users' benefit, rather than promoting the product's virtues and innovation. If the product can provide significant cost savings to clients (e.g. a pay-back period under two years), this translates to a significant user benefit.

- Determine the potential client's interest in your product or service. This interest can be demonstrated by letters of support or appreciation.

- New products or services can be offered as prototypes to potential users selling at or below cost in exchange for benefit feedback and endorsements.

- Document booking orders with supporting data indicating the number of customers who have committed to purchase. This allows you to provide a convincing projection of the "rate of acceptance" for the product or service, and the pace at which it is likely to be sold.

2. ANTICIPATE INVESTORS' OR LENDERS' REQUIREMENTS

Investors:

➤ Who are your potential investors? Are they friends and family, angels, venture capitalists or strategic corporate investors?

➤ Understand the investors' primary objectives. These can be summarized as follows:

♦ Exit strategy (cashing out). Investors do not expect to receive a steady flow of dividends from small, fast-growing companies. Their return will be the profit gained from a successful exit either by selling their appreciated share holdings once the company goes public or by redeeming shareholdings once the company is sold.

♦ The price and relative percentage ownership. The potential value of the company is usually based on projected earnings (EBIT) or cash flow (EBITDA) five years into the future, in conjunction with an appropriate earnings or cash flow multiple. The relative percentage shareholding derived will mirror the investor's required rate of return which, in turn, reflects the risk of the venture.

Examples:

A company with new products and unproven management: 40%+ annual returns are usually required.

A company with developed products and proven management: 25% to 35% annual returns are usually required.

➤ Provide evidence of a strong proprietary position (i.e., patents, copyrights, trademarks in place).

➤ Detail the use and specific allocation of the investors' proceeds.

Lenders

Remember the WARS acronym (Chapter 11 – Financing):

➤ Why is financing required?

➤ Amount of funds required?

➤ Repayment: over what timeline and from what source (ongoing earnings or sale of assets?)

➤ Security: what company assets are available?

Does the lender have a clearly defined 'alternate way out' and would this involve the provision of personal guarantees?

3. EMPHASIZE MANAGEMENT DEPTH

Does your management team have:

- Proven industry experience?
- Previous start-up experience?
- A track record in successfully bringing new products or services to market?

4. CLEARLY DEFINE YOUR CUSTOMERS AND COMPETITORS

Customers

- Segmentation – Which are the most attractive segments?
- Targeting – Who is buying from you?
- Preferences – What do they buy from you?
- Timing – When do they buy?
- Criteria – Why do they buy?

Competition

- Demonstrate your knowledge of the competition and how you are keeping track of them (latest product offerings, price discounts, etc.) on an ongoing basis.

5. OBTAIN FEEDBACK

Show drafts of your business plan to business advisors, senior management and other key employees. Ensure that your lawyer has confirmed that the plan meets all necessary regulatory issues (especially from an investment standpoint).

6. PREPARE REALISTIC FINANCIAL PROJECTIONS

- Investors and lenders will focus on the accuracy and integrity of your financial numbers.
- Projections and revenues, gross margins and earnings have to be carefully supported by assumptions that are reasonable and that can be defended.
- Complete 'best expected/worst case' scenarios. You can be sure that your numbers will be stress tested by the investors or lenders.

7. COMPLETE THE EXECUTIVE SUMMARY (LAST)

This is the most important section of your Business Plan. People will read it first and formulate their initial impressions based on these critical pages. If you do not get the potential investor's attention with the Executive Summary, they will likely not read the rest of the business plan.

Your ERS can usually be fine tuned to meet the information requirements of the Executive Summary.

FIVE WAYS TO TORPEDO A BUSINESS PLAN

1. Infatuation with the special features of products or services (internal focus) versus demonstrating awareness of marketplace needs (external focus).

2. Unrealistic financial projections. No sensitivity analysis. No correlation with industry norms and benchmarks.

3. Lack of information on key management, or unexplained gaps in resumes.

4. Spreadsheet overkill, with excessive analysis and scenarios creating a numerical 'smog' that deters and confuses the reader.

5. Delegating the business plan preparation to outsiders. Business owners sometimes borrow heavily from sample business plans or delegate the complete task to outside consultants.

   It is critical that the key elements of the plan be prepared by the company management team (not just the founder). External resources can be engaged to fine tune and complete the final plan documents.

PACKAGING AND PRESENTATION TIPS

The Business Plan provides outsiders (investors, lenders) with a first impression of your company and its management team. The following tips will assist you in presenting a professional and effective package to your audience.

APPEARANCE

> Professional binding and printing are important. Avoid a too lavish or glossy appearance, which might be misinterpreted (excessive spending? snow job?).

> The cover should bear the company's name, address, and date issued. Maintain strict copy numbers (maximum 20). This allows you to keep track of the number of copies circulated.

> Length: We suggest 25 to 30 pages maximum. Again, a carefully prepared Executive Summary (maximum two to three pages) is crucial in convincing the reader to proceed with the rest of the document.

> Background and supporting information can be included in an additional binder that would be available as part of the due diligence process.

PRESENTATION

> Wherever possible, obtain an appointment with your prospective audience and get face to face when delivering the Business Plan. This strategy allows you to highlight the opportunity in person. Keep the meeting brief and leave the plan for the reader to review at their own leisure.

> Clearly identify the person who provided you with the opportunity to meet your audience (your lawyer, accountant, etc.).

> A more formal presentation, perhaps involving a panel of investors, could involve a brief PowerPoint presentation (maximum 20 slides) which summarizes the key elements of the plan. (Refer to Chapter 9.)

Note:

- Slides should be in bullet form with short and concise sentences (maximum six per slide) in order to retain the audience's attention.

- Always rehearse this type of presentation.

- Set up the presentation equipment early and test it.

- Have back-up overhead slides and a projector just in case 'Murphy's Law' strikes.

USEFUL WEB SITES

www.americanexpresss.com	Creating an effective business plan
www.morebusiness.com	Business and marketing plan templates
www.bplans.com	Comprehensive business planning tools including a Plan Wizard that matches sample plans to your business

SECTION 5

CASE STUDY

THE INN ON CORTES ISLAND
EXPANSION CHALLENGES
& OPPORTUNITIES

INTRODUCTION

Another crisp fall morning brought a refreshing breeze in from across the Pacific Ocean. It was mid October 2004 and as he paused to look out to sea, at the halfway mark of his daily jog, Jonathan Walker wondered whether he would ever realize his expansion plans at the Inn on Cortes Island.

Since its grand opening two years ago, most of his energies had been spent managing the operational and human resources aspects of the organization. These challenges had become increasingly more complex, and were complicated by a recent decision to launch an aggressive expansion of the resort.

TOURISM IN BRITISH COLUMBIA

Tourism within British Columbia had become one of the most important industries in the province, growing steadily and rapidly since the World Fair, Expo '86, showcased the beauty of Vancouver and BC to the world. By 2000, annual tourism revenue in the province totaled nearly $10 billion, with 22.5 million overnight visitors[1]. British Columbia's main markets for tourism were BC's own residents, visitors from other parts of Canada, and visitors from international locations, most importantly the United States, Asia, and Europe.

The events of September 11, 2001 had a devastating effect on tourism around the world and in particular B.C. In 2003, Canadian tourism experienced further difficulties with the escalation of the Iraq war, the SARS outbreak in Ontario, and the West Nile virus which all combined to bring unwelcome international attention to Canada. Total tourism revenues fell by 2%, to $50.8 billion, while in British Columbia, 2003 tourism revenues had fallen to $8.9 billion.[2]

Human Resources issues in played a major role within the B.C tourism industry with a strong perception that tourism jobs did not pay well, along with challenges associated with recruitment, retaining workers, and training/development issues. A significant related concern was the tendency for tourism businesses to promote from within, which often launched employees into management positions without any preparatory training in business skills or supervising others.

THE INN ON CORTES ISLAND

Cortes Island is about 25 km long, 13 km wide and 13,000 hectares in area with the southern half lying in the rain shadow of Vancouver Island, creating a drier climate than the northern half of the island. Most of the island's population lives on the southern end, graced with Arbutus and Manzanita trees that cling to imposing bleached granite bluffs.

Cortes Island (pronounced Cortez) and nearby Hernando Island were named after the Spanish conqueror of Mexico, Hernando Cortes. The Spanish cartographer, Valdez, who charted the local waters in 1793, established this unusual link. The Spanish never settled the area, but Cortes and other Spanish names remained.

The island is located on the northern end of the Strait of Georgia, between Campbell River on central Vancouver Island and the mainland coast of British Columbia and is accessed via ferry from Heriot Bay on the east coast of Quadra Island.[3] The Inn on Cortes Island (ICI) was located just outside the hamlet of Squirrel's Landing, an anchorage facing Desolation Sound.

Two years prior to the Inn's opening in March of 2002, Jonathan Walker had been vacationing on Cortes Island, taking a well-earned break from his successful financial management company. Wanting to really get away from it all, he decided to investigate the area and immediately fell in love with the ruggedly beautiful setting.

During the trip, acting on an impulse, Jonathan acquired an 8-acre parcel of land that had been in foreclosure. He felt the setting had great development potential and after closing the property purchase, he commenced a complex rezoning process, which involved the local council, the federal Fisheries department, and the Islands Trust.

It took almost one year to obtain all of the necessary approvals. With the rezoning process complete, Jonathan worked closely with his accountants and tourism industry consultants to undertake a detailed feasibility analysis, prior to commencing construction.

Based on the appraised value of the project, on a completion basis, he was able to secure $3 million financing for the $6 million construction project, with the balance funded by a $3.5 million equity contribution from Jonathan (cash and the clear title property). After only one year of construction, the Inn opened for business in March 2002.

Jonathan's vision for the resort was realized – situated right on the beachfront, each of the 28 rooms faced the water, with lapping waves seen and heard from all balconies. The rooms all featured Jacuzzi tubs, fireplaces, DVD/CD players, and high quality linens. The interiors had been completed in a theme of earth tones, and featured paintings and prints done by local artists. A gourmet restaurant and bar completed the experience, allowing guests to choose from a wide variety of fresh, local food without having to venture away from the resort. Not a single corner had been cut in creating a resort experience with a focus on excellence.

In terms of market positioning, the ICI was depicted as a comfortable and elegant "boutique inn" experience for an upscale clientele. A sophisticated web site presence was built which accurately reflected the spirit of the relaxed setting. Recognizing the value of repeat business, marketing efforts were focused on developing and retaining a loyal clientele who would be willing to return to the Inn, and to refer friends and colleagues as well.

A media-consulting firm was engaged to initiate a 'soft opening' strategy of press releases and industry familiarization (FAM) tours, resulting in favorable publicity, prior to and soon after, opening their doors for business.

ORGANIZATIONAL STRUCTURE

Jonathan was in his early 40s, single and had extensive business interests in nearby Vancouver. He was the sole shareholder and CEO of the ICI but had a General Manager to oversee the day-to-day operations. The resort had four main functional areas: front desk, housekeeping, maintenance and grounds, and food services. Each department had its own manager.

To prepare for the opening in 2002, a mother and son team had been hired into the two most prominent positions at the Inn: Anna was brought on as the General Manager, and her son, Lloyd became the Chef. Both had extensive experience working in a high-end pub in the English Lake District and appeared to be a close knit and effective team.

However, after 18 months of operations, it became apparent that this 'family team' was not working effectively – there had been a litany of operational and HR problems which seemed to flare up without warning. Resolving these issues became both stressful and time-consuming for Jonathan as he juggled his various corporate and ownership responsibilities.

After considerable deliberation, the mother and son management team were terminated one stormy November night. In protest, several other members of the staff resigned at the same time. Jonathan commented:

> " Here I was in midst of a cold and wet November with no management support and three other outraged staff also marching out of the door. Luckily, the consulting firm that I had used to assess the Inn's initial feasibility was able to provide some solid professional advice to source a new GM and replacement staff for the resort."

Within a few weeks, Edward Bourgogne, an experienced, no-nonsense manager of European heritage was hired. To replace the departed chef, Edward hired Jackie Daniels. Coming to ICI with impeccable training and some good experience, she was a better kitchen manager than Lloyd had been, and she got on very well with the kitchen staff team. Edward resolved to give her a chance to develop into a "star" chef that would focus additional attention on the resort and enhance its reputation.

CUSTOMER PROFILE

The Inn was open year round with the late spring, summer and early fall being the strongest revenue season. Despite the inclement B.C. winter weather, a secondary 'storm watching' season had evolved with couples seeking escape from their busy urban environments, to enjoy the warmth and shelter of the Inn while it was pounded by strong winds out of the south east.

The primary profile of the visitors to the Inn could best be described as affluent middle class couples, taking a long weekend or couple of weeks, to recharge in a pristine, secluded environment. There was also an interesting trend towards family weddings where the Inn would be taken over for a whole weekend to accommodate the event. While a strong cash flow generator, there had been some push back from 'regular' clients who sometimes were unable to book for a return trip on their desired weekend.

Jonathan also felt that there was potential for more family style vacations and had been investigating the merits of adding high end cabin style accommodations to serve the 'three generation' boomer families that were now seeking to travel together.

THE COMPETITION

Despite the unique ambience of the Inn, there were a few upscale competing operations both on Cortes, and on nearby Quadra Island.

On Cortes, the world-renowned Hollyhock retreat resort had built a strong reputation for quality with its ocean-side private rooms and more rustic dorm rooms built in an earthy West Coast style. It was further differentiated with unique tent sites, complete with a cedar bathhouse, which made camping feel like a luxury. (www. hollyhock.ca)

On Quadra Island, April Point Resort (www.aprilpoint.com) had also built a formidable reputation as a desirable resort location, offering glorious sunset views over the ocean channel across to nearby Campbell River. The resort was a 10-minute water taxi ride from the main Island, and had positioned itself as an upscale fishing lodge, offering a mix of adventure and relaxation for couples, families, groups, and anglers of all ages.

There were also a number of Cortes based smaller, 'funkier' operations, more down market than the ICI, who actually collaborated with each other and the resort, especially during the peak seasons when double bookings sometimes occurred.

OPERATIONS AND HR ISSUES

In the fall of 2004, the Inn employed 30 permanent staff complemented by an additional 10 summer season employees. The four department managers – front desk, housekeeping, maintenance and grounds, food services – all reported directly to Edward Bourgogne. Since the resort opened, staff turnover had been a critical issue, despite the provision of on-site staff housing right at the resort. Jonathan reflected:

> 'In the beginning, initial staff hiring and training had been completed quickly but faced with the relatively isolated rural area of Cortes, there was only a small local population from which to hire, so we had to source a high number of staff from outside of the area. We thought that staff housing was the solution but we continued to lose staff on a regular basis.
>
> With Edward coming on board six months ago, the situation has stabilized somewhat. He seems to possess decent leadership and inter-personal skills, although, just last week, he and Jackie had a major altercation over menu items, which has evolved into a rather troubling feud. I am not sure how to resolve this issue and I sense that the kitchen staff are becoming more truculent and distant from their colleagues.'

FINANCIAL PERFORMANCE

First year projected revenues were $2.2 million, based on expected occupancy of 64% and an average room rate of $225.00. Actual results came in close to plan with a small operating loss recorded.

In the following year, revenues increased by 10% reflecting stable occupancy and higher off-season rates as the storm watching weekends came into vogue. Profitability still remained elusive due to higher than anticipated marketing costs and staff severance packages that had to be funded during the year.

The latest interim financials showed improved performance against plan (both revenue and profitability), which Jonathan greeted with relief and optimism as he contemplated his resort expansion plans.

From a Balance Sheet perspective, the company was reasonably well capitalized. Amicable relations with the First National Bank were reported despite some recent overdue term loan payments and unforeseen overdrafts. Jonathan commented:

> *'The First National were enormously supportive when we put together our first construction financing package for $3 million and also extended an operating line of $500,000 to us as well. However, over the past few months, we have been at the limit of the credit line.*
>
> *We are experiencing tightening cash flow despite just completing the summer season and our apparent strong interim profit performance. I am mystified by this phenomenon and worry that relations may be getting strained with the bank – incredibly poor timing as we meet soon to request increased financing for our cabin expansion.*
>
> *On a more positive note, we continue to receive very positive reviews from our clients who are becoming huge fans of our upscale dining room and world-class menu. I attribute these accolades to our decision last year to substantially expand our wine cellar with more selections from B.C. wineries and Chile. Of course, from a financial standpoint, this is also very positive news, as we derive excellent gross margins from our wine sales.'*

THE EXPANSION PLANS

Over a few glasses of exquisite Marley Farms 2003 Pinot Grigio, Jonathan and Edward had resolved to press ahead with the cabin expansion. Edward had also pushed hard for the development of a full service luxury spa facility but this was temporarily shelved due to the projected cost ($750K) to set up such an operation. Buoyed by the encouraging interim financial results, Jonathan decided to put forth a brief financing request to the Bank, summarized as follows:

The resort expansion would consist of 15 luxury cabins with an estimated cost of $110K per cabin for a total of $1,650K. The cost estimate included both hard (construction and fittings) and soft (architect, design) costs.

Bank financing was requested for $1.8 million that included an additional $150K to cover working capital needs during the six months construction period.

Jonathan reflected optimistically:

> *'While I have a number of internal challenges, especially on the HR side, I feel that the timing is right to undertake the cabin expansion, as part of our differentiation strategy. It is going to be a tough sell to the bank but I feel that we can make a compelling case.*
>
> *The first thing we need to do is get a current fix on our present corporate health, by considering both our external environment and also our internal operations. I also need to resolve our staff turnover problems and address the deteriorating relationship between Edward and Jackie.*
>
> *Then, we need to put a financing application package together for the bank and demonstrate our capability to generate positive, sustained cash flow to service and repay the debt – our revenue and earnings projections will have to withstand intense scrutiny by the bank!'*

As he turned back towards the resort to finish his morning run, he began to anticipate the next steps in moving from the planning stage to the actual resort expansion.

THE NEXT STEPS

1. Based on the case and accompanying financial statements/ratio analysis, use the following 'size up' work sheets to complete an External and Internal evaluation of the ICI operations.

2. Prepare a 3-4 page Enterprise Review Summary (ERS) that summarizes the financing requirements associated with the cabin expansion.

3. Based on your overall assessment of the ICI resort and its future prospects, should Jonathan proceed with the expansion at this time?

REFERENCES

1. *Starting A Tourism Business.* Tourism British Columbia, 2003.

2. British Columbia Tourism Top Ten Facts. *Tourism BC,* 2004. (http://www.tourism.bc.ca/template.asp?id=10)

3. Cortes Island reference (www.Vancouverisland.com)

Exhibit 1

Statement of Income & Retained Earnings (Unaudited)

Inn on Cortes Island Ltd
STATEMENT OF INCOME AND RETAINED EARNINGS
For the Year Ended March 31st

	2003	2004	Interim - 6 months
Revenues			
Rooms	1380	1518	860
Food and beverage	828	911	512
	$ 2208	$ 2429	$ 1372
Departmental expenses			
Rooms	516	543	260
Food and beverage	636	730	420
	$ 1152	$ 1273	$ 680
Departmental Gross Profit	$ 1056	$ 1156	$ 692
Undistributed expenses			
Administration and general	267	289	141
Marketing	198	218	106
Utilities	34	44	25
Maintenance	28	34	17
	$ 527	$ 585	$ 289
Income before fixed charges	$ 529	$ 571	$ 403
Fixed expenses			
Property and business taxes	78	96	45
Insurance	45	56	27
Provision for capital replacement	50	55	
	173	207	72
Income available for debt service	$ 356	$ 364	$ 331
Depreciation	292	277	145
Bank Interest	214	207	109
Net Income before Tax	$ -150	$ -120	$ 77
Income Taxes			24
Net Income	$ -150	$ -120	$ 53

NOTES TO STATEMENTS

Rooms:

- ➤ Revenues relate to room sales usually paid for by charge card.

- ➤ Expenses include staff wages/benefits, cable, laundry, guest services and travel agent commissions.

Food & Beverage:

- ➤ Revenues consist of Food ($660K), Beer ($30K), Wine ($195K) and Liquor ($26K) sales.

- ➤ Expenses consisted of Cost of Sales – $346K (average 38%), and Departmental expenses – primarily wages and operating supplies.

- ➤ The operating losses for the first two years – $150K and $120K – were attributed by Jonathan to higher than forecast marketing expenses.

Exhibit 2

Balance Sheet (Unaudited)

The Inn on Cortes Island Ltd.
BALANCE SHEETS (Unaudited)
For the Year Ended March 31 $000's

		2003		2004
ASSETS				
Current Assets				
Cash	$	5	$	4
Accounts Receivable		65		137
Inventories		230		367
Prepaid Expenses		5		4
Total Current Assets	$	305	$	512
Fixed Assets				
Land	$	750	$	750
Buldings		4838		4596
Less Accumulated Depreciation		-242		-230
		4596		4366
Furnishings & Equipment		890		845
Less Accumulated Depreciation		-45		-42
		845		803
Computers		90		85
Less Accumulated Depreciation		-5		-5
		85		80
Total Fixed Assets	$	6276	$	5999
Total Assets	$	6581	$	6511
LIABILITIES				
Current Liabilities				
Bank Overdraft	$	27	$	104
Accounts Payable		154		101
Customer Deposits		50		76
Current Portion of Long-term Debt				150
Total Current Liabilities	$	231	$	431
Long-term Liabilities				
Bank term loan	$	3000	$	2850
Shareholder loan J.W Holdings Inc		2750		2750
Total Liabilities		5981		6031
SHAREHOLDERS' EQUITY				
Share Capital	$	750	$	750
Retained Earnings		-150		-270
Total Shareholders' Equity		600		480
Total Liabilities & Shareholder Equity	$	6581	$	6511

NOTES TO THE BALANCE SHEET

> Accounts Receivable – relates to outstanding payments from wedding receptions/conferences with increase in 2004 $70K primarily due to B.C Vintners retreat with payment in full promised by calendar year end.

> Inventories – 2004: Food supplies $154K , Beer & Wine supplies $200K, increase year over year primarily due to $120K shipment of Chilean vintage wines.

> Fixed Assets – the resort property was independently appraised for bank financing purposes at $7.2 million in April 2002.

> Shareholder loan – due to Jonathan's holding company with proceeds contributed towards the cost of the resort construction and subrogated (postponed) to the bank. The postponement allows this liability to be restated as equity for ratio calculation purposes.

Exhibit 3

Revenue and Expense Projections

The Inn on Cortes Island Ltd.
BALANCE SHEETS (Unaudited)
For the Year Ended March 31 $000's

	2005	2006
Rooms		
Number of rooms	28	28
Average Room Rate	$ 229.00	$ 233.00
Occupancy	70.0%	75.0%
Room Nights Available	10,220	10,220
Room Nights Sold	7,154	7,665
Cabins		
Average Room Rate		$ 136.00
Occupancy		70.0%
Number of rooms		15
Room Nights Available		5,475
Room Nights Sold		3,832
Revenues		
Rooms	$ 1,645	$ 1,785
Food and beverage	990	1,070
Cabins	-	520
Total	2,635	3,375
Departmental expenses		
Rooms	615	660
Food and beverage	762	824
Cabins	-	182
Total	1,377	1,666
Departmental gross profit	1,258	1,709
Undistributed expenses		
Administration and general	295	325
Marketing	180	240
Utilities	50	70
Maintenance	40	55
	565	690
Income before fixed charges	693	1,019
Fixed expenses		
Property and business taxes	125	135
Insurance	65	75
Provision for capital replacement	50	50
	240	260
Income available for debt service	$ 453	$ 759
Forecast annual Term loan payments		464
Coverage		**1.64**

NOTES TO PROJECTED REVENUES AND EXPENSES

> Jonathan's accountants prepared the two year forecasts based on detailed discussions with Edward and his senior staff. A sensitivity analysis was completed with three scenarios examined – best, expected and worst case. The forecast presented here is the 'expected case'.

> The bank was presented with a detailed package of supporting materials including revenue and cost breakdowns for the Rooms, F& B and Cabin components.

> Revenues and Expenses associated with the Inn core operations – Rooms and F&B were forecast on the basis of the encouraging interim results to September 2004.

> The Cabin forecast Revenues were based upon the completion of 15 units within a four month construction window. A nightly room rate of $136 was selected, based upon other similar operations on Vancouver Island. A modest 70% occupancy rate was chosen for the first year.

> The bank term debt is forecast at $4.8 million, with $1.8 million additional financing covering the cabin hard and soft construction costs.

> Annual principal and interest payments are forecast at $38,700 per month, based on a 20 year amortization and a fixed interest rate of 7.5%.

> The resultant debt service coverage is a comfortable 1.64x – if the amortization is redued to 15 years, the coverage reduces to approx. 1.42x.

> An updated Appraisal has been completed, rendering an increased valuation of $9.3 million which reflects the $1.8 million cabin expansion. Proposed bank term debt ($4.8 million) will be 52% of the appraised value.

Exhibit 4

Historical Ratio Analysis

INN ON CORTES ISLAND LTD
RATIO ANALYSIS HISTORICAL & FORECAST 2003 TO 2006

(thousands of dollars)

	2003	2004	2005 forecast	2006 forecast
Gross Revenues	2208	2,429	2,635	3,375
GPM	48%	48%	48%	51%
EBITDA	356	364	453	759
Working Capital	74	81		
Current ratio	1.32	1.2		
Debt: Equity ratio	0.96	1.02		
Total Debt/EBITDA	9.08	9.01		
Inventory turns	132 days	184 days		
A/R Collection	10 days	21 days		
Revenue Growth		10%	8%	28%

Exhibit 5
Area Map and
Photographs of the Inn

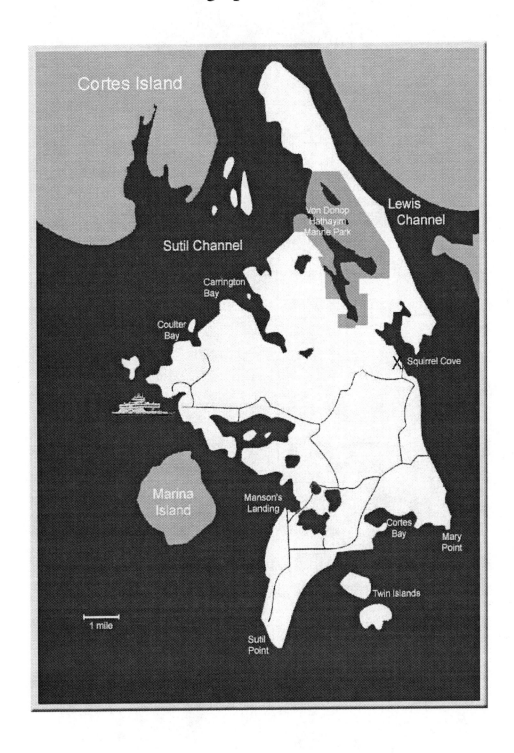

THE BUSINESS ENVIRONMENT

	Opportunities	Threats
Political		
Economic		
Societal		
Technological		

INDUSTRY CONDITIONS

Competitive Conditions

	High	Neutral	Low
Threat of new entrants			
Bargaining power of customers			
Bargaining power of suppliers			
Threat of substitutes			
Intensity of competition			

Key success factors

FINANCIAL SIZE-UP

	Strengths	Weaknesses
Profitability and Cash Flow		
Liquidity		
Stability		
Efficiency		
Growth		

Action items

MARKETING SIZE-UP

	Strengths	Weaknesses
MARKET TACTICS Price Product Place Promotion		
MARKET ANALYSIS Segmentation Competition Competitive Advantage Customer Needs		
MARKET STRATEGY EXECUTION		

Action items

OPERATIONS SIZE-UP

	Strengths	Weaknesses
Operations process		
Risk management issues		
Legal issues		
Location issues		

Action items

HUMAN RESOURCES SIZE-UP

	Strengths	Weaknesses
Human Resource function Recruitment and Hiring Training and Development Compensation, Performance and Incentives		
Leadership issues Organizational Structure Skills Development Teams and Teamwork Management Capabilities		

Action items

TECHNOLOGY SIZE-UP

	Strengths	Weaknesses
Current I.T. infrastructure in place		
Intellectual property issues		
Potential risk factors		

Action items

APPENDIX 1

EXTERNAL AND INTERNAL 'SIZE-UP'

THE INN ON CORTES ISLAND LTD

THE BUSINESS ENVIRONMENT

	Opportunities	Threats
Political	A complex re-zoning process has been undertaken with credibility built with local municipal authorities. Pro-tourism provincial government with strong focus to help on-going industry recovery efforts..	Are there additional rezoning requirements for the proposed cabin expansion?
Economic	Tourism is still a growth sector in spite of recent issues encountered in the industry. Greater 'boomer' disposable income as family 'nests' empty?	Vacations are threatened by economic downturns – one of the first "luxuries" to go.
Societal	ICI's main regional market is the growing baby-boomer segment – easiest to access with internet marketing efforts. ICI is well positioned to take advantage of growing meetings and conferences demand as organizations recognize need to re-invigorate employees.	Consumers still "skittish" about travel given the events of September 11th, SARS, the Iraq war, BSE, and the B.C forest fires. Not enough skilled labour in the Cortes area as young people leave for higher paying jobs in Vancouver and Victoria.
Technological	Web-based marketing not yet fully explored by ICI – can be very lucrative especially to independent operators. Potential to use POS systems to more accurately track guest activities at the Lodge and leverage this information in customer relation management efforts.	

INDUSTRY CONDITIONS

Competitive Conditions

	High	Neutral	Low
Threat of new entrants The prohibitive costs of starting up a competing resort on the Island (financial and regulatory) are a strong barrier to entry.			X
Bargaining power of customers Many accommodation options are available to well heeled travelers, especially in the 'long weekend' market segment.	X		
Bargaining power of suppliers Food & Beverages: few supplier options in such a small community allied with a 'two ferry' trip to deliver supplies. Labour: high local turnover due to lower wages and perceived lack of opportunity	X		
Threat of substitutes Many accommodations options are available in the market, though few offer the specific features boasted by ICI: remote and rugged beauty couple with comfort and luxury		X	
Intensity of competition Local are operators are more collaborative than competitive, though access to qualified staff is still a 'competitive' issue.		X	

Key success factors

- ➤ Hands-on ownership.
- ➤ High level of guest care.
- ➤ Unique product and location plus casual, comfortable luxury.
- ➤ Already enjoys repeat business.

FINANCIAL SIZE-UP

	Strengths	Weaknesses
Profitability and Cash Flow	Latest interim F/S point to improved revenue and earnings performance	Despite a strong take –off in revenue growth, the Inn has experienced two successive years of operating losses. Cash generation performance is weak evidence by increasing A/R and Inventory levels over the past year.
Liquidity		Thin working capital position evidenced by the 1.2 current ratio that has declined over the past year. Inventories are a major component of current assets – largely consist of the recently acquired vintage Chilean wine collection.
Stability	Stable Debt: Equity ratio in 1:1 range once the J.W Holdings shareholder loan is 'added back' to equity due to the postponement to the bank.	Disconcerting Total Debt: EBITDA ratio (9.0 range), which would be a significant 'red flashing light' to the bank. Based on the latest EBITDA results, it would take 9 years to retire the existing debt load – the usual comfort level is < 4.0
Efficiency		The resort is carrying too high a level of A/R in what is supposed to be a 'cash business' – this has become a serious drag on cash generation performance. The Inventory levels are also far too high with an excessive focus on building a 'fine wine' selection.
Growth	An impressive first two years from a revenue performance standpoint. Further steady growth forecast as the cabin expansion gets underway.	Poor profitability performance in the first two years – while interim statements show a welcome re-bound, these are 'in-house' and may require adjustment at year-end.

MARKETING SIZE-UP

	Strengths	**Weaknesses**
MARKET TACTICS		
Price	High perceived value for guests compared to other (smaller and funkier) operators in the area.	Can prices be set higher without adverse effect upon occupancy rates? Have the proposed cabin prices been market tested to ensure realism?
Product	Couples and families are both accommodated by addition of cabins. Great food on site keeps guests close by: potential "captive audience" for a future spa?	Vulnerable to "back of house" H-R problems spilling over and disrupting guests' experiences.
Place	Simple 'distribution channel' with delivery of a top tier accommo-dation and dining experience on site.	Remote location limits access to casual travelers and any last minute 'buying decisions'.
Promotion	"Soft-sell" approach, collabora-tive with other operators in the area has been successful.	Can leverage technological op-tions to target more international clientele via web-based initiatives?
MARKET ANALYSIS		
Segmentation		Detailed segmentation analysis for existing and new target markets is needed, especially for the new cabin segment.
Competition	Apparent collaborative relation-ship with local competition, which is sparse on Cortes and Quadra Islands.	Other high end resorts on Vancouver Island will compete more in the future especially when they focus on the 'two ferry' ride factor.
Competitive Advantage	Unique location, strong strategic and operational management with access to expansion funding.	
Customer Needs		Are more family related activities needed, and will the cabin expansion address this need?
MARKET STRATEGY EXECUTION		Need to develop a go-forward marketing plan to leverage ICI's initial success and planned cabin expansion. To include a detailed segmentation analysis of the existing and proposed target markets.

OPERATIONS SIZE-UP

	Strengths	Weaknesses
Operations process	Recent improvements in kitchen procedures with arrival of Jackie Daniels.	Is there potential for bench marking practices in the room and F&B areas? Seasonality issues – staff scheduling as the seasonal demand changes?
Risk management issues	Succession issues – Jonathan is relatively young and in good health (he likes running but also imbibes his fair share of the grape). Key person and disability insurance should be considered for both Jonathan and Edward.	Does the resort have the following in place: A formal Risk Management system? An Emergency Preparedness program? A Health & Safety program for staff? An Environmental Sustainability program?
Legal issues	Effective legal counsel appears to be in place given the successful financing and completion of the resort.	
Location issues		Remote location means guest access and travel delay issues. There is also high supplier power due to their access issues. Utilities servicing is more difficult.

HUMAN RESOURCES SIZE-UP

	Strengths	Weaknesses
Human Resource function		
Recruitment and Hiring		Need dedicated effort and planning, given limited local pool of workers.
Training and Development		A formal Training and Development program would likely contribute to employee retention.
Compensation, Performance and Incentives		Are supervisors and management properly recognizing employees?
		Is there potential for profit sharing?
		Is Edward being properly incented?
Leadership issues		
Organizational Structure	Effective, experienced GM now in place. Appears to have a close working relationship with JW?	
Skills Development	Jonathan has had good access to professional hospitality industry consultants who had the expertise necessary to create ICI.	Minimal employee expertise to run the Lodge day-to-day operations?
Teams and Teamwork		Cliques have formed in different staff departments, especially the kitchen. There appears to be a lack of overall teamwork.
Management Capabilities		Jonathan is still relatively new to hospitality industry and therefore very dependent upon his GM.
		Edward and Jackie tensions need to be resolved quickly – how would this be accomplished?

INFORMATION TECHNOLOGY SIZE-UP

	Strengths	Weaknesses
Current IT infrastructure	Guest experience is as modern as possible with Internet access in all rooms, cable TV, movies, CD players etc.	Potential to use available CRM software Tools ?
Intellectual property issues		Needs to investigate Trademark and Copyright issues with regard to the resort name and logo?
Potential risk factors		Future capital investment requirements to up-keep the IT infrastructure?

APPENDIX 2

ENTERPRISE REVIEW SUMMARY (ERS)

FOR

THE INN ON CORTES ISLAND LTD

ENTERPRISE REVIEW SUMMARY

OVERVIEW

This report has been prepared in conjunction with management to obtain additional financing to expand and improve operations at The Inn on Cortes Island (ICI). The financing request is for $1.8 million to cover expansion costs to complete 15 luxury cabins adjacent to the main resort lodge. The new funding includes soft and hard costs to complete construction plus $150,000 for working capital requirements. This new funding plus existing term debt of $3 million will result in a total term debt of $4.8 million.

An updated appraisal has been completed with a value of $9.3 million derived on a completion basis. Grant Thornton's tourism consulting group has been engaged to complete an updated industry analysis and cash flow projection in support of this request.

COMPANY DESCRIPTION

Jonathan Walker is the sole shareholder of ICI, which was founded in 2002. Walker purchased the 8-acre parcel on Cortez Island and invested substantial personal capital of $3.5 million to construct a 28-room boutique resort lodge complete with gourmet dining room and lounge. This exclusive waterfront property is located on the northern end of the Strait of Georgia, between Campbell River on central Vancouver Island and the mainland coast of British Columbia (see map). It is accessed by B.C. Ferries on their daily island routes.

The lodge was designed to capture the rugged beauty of BC's west coast and targets discerning affluent upper middle class travelers seeking a unique retreat experience. Every room enjoys a private balcony overlooking spectacular ocean vistas at nature's edge. Inn patrons experience a unique dining experience and a world-class wine cellar under the purview of signature chef, Jackie Daniels.

ICI has gained a loyal following since opening and promotes itself primarily through a sophisticated web site and referrals of satisfied guests. Initial marketing efforts were more costly using a media consulting firm and industry familiarization tours (FAMs) to gain awareness, however this strategy has helped ICI to sustain revenues and avoid costly commissions to booking agencies.

The resort lodge is open year round at an average 70% occupancy, which is exceptional for this new and exclusive facility, a testament to the guest experience and service provided. An emerging market for the "Storm Watching" shoulder season will further enhance occupancy rates.

CURRENT BUSINESS AND INDUSTRY ENVIRONMENT

Tourism is one of the most prominent industries in British Columbia. At its peak in 2000, annual tourism revenues in the province totaled nearly 10 billion with 22.5 million overnight visitors. British Columbia's main markets for tourism, includes local residents, visitors from other parts of Canada and visitors from International locations, most importantly the United States, Asia and Europe. While the events of September 11, 2001 and outbreaks of SARS and the West Nile virus dampened tourism revenues, recent activity indicates growth has rebounded. Moreover, the 2010 Olympic games in Whistler are expected to create a strong awareness and International draw to "supernatural" BC.

The industry is sensitive to economic cycles largely driven by business and consumer confidence and increases in household disposable income. In Canada, there is an increasing demand for specialty business properties located on urban fringe areas with characteristics reflecting consumer desire for a unique eco tourism experience. The threat of new entrants and availability of waterfront properties is limited.

A complimentary concentration of resorts lies within close proximity to ICI, each with distinct, unique offerings. An opportunity exists to share supply procurement and joint marketing efforts and to continue the cooperative relationships that exist for referring overbooked clients.

PRODUCTS/SERVICES

In two short years, ICI has garnered a loyal client following while a secondary market of small groups, such as wedding parties, has also emerged. ICI could also accommodate small group corporate retreats if it had more room capacity.

The hospitality industry demands regular reinvestment to maintain guest satisfaction and sustain and grow revenue streams. Walker has astutely "phased in" amenities, as cash flow and profitability will allow. An investment of $120,000 was made in wine inventories to build to maintain standards commensurate with this upper end segment. The wine sales also provide for attractive gross profit margins.

The expansion of room capacity is a logical next move and is necessary to ensure ICI is able to satisfy its expanding base of loyal repeat customers. A proven occupancy has been established and the resort could enjoy further efficiencies by utilizing its land base for more density. The cabin expansion plan will also fulfill several strategic objectives including the further differentiation among resorts within its existing market segment.

Also, Walker has identified a new segment of "three generation" boomer families that are seeking to travel together where cabin facilities would be ideal. Finally, having cabins apart from the main lodge will provide guests extra privacy and allow for more room capacity for group functions without mixing client segments.

MARKET SEGMENTATION AND COMPETITOR EVALUATION

The primary market segment is affluent long weekend and vacation travelers seeking distinctive quality with enhanced dining and retreat experience. Attraction is primarily Canadian with a growing International component. The most prominent visitor would be American, due to the close proximity, favorable exchange and safe haven pristine appeal of the B.C. west coast.

The industry segment can be defined as destination waterfront specialty boutique style independent operator. There may be an opportunity to gain significant international exposure and recognition if ICI were able to acquire a designation as a 'Relais Chateaux' inn (www.relaischateaux.com) The designation is accorded to high quality independent and distinctive resorts worldwide and is a recognized standard.

ICI is well positioned in the market having taken full advantage of its premier waterfront property and location, while successfully attracting and delivering the value proposition to the affluent traveler seeking a "retreat" experience.

MANAGEMENT

Walker possesses a strong financial background and proven business acumen evidenced by the success of his other business ventures. He has successfully engaged business professionals to complete feasibility studies, and to set up marketing, legal and accounting infrastructure.

Walker has also paid particular attention to staffing the key position of General Manager, making one interim change since inception. The current manager, Edward Bourgogne, is well regarded as an experienced, no-nonsense manager of European heritage. His leadership and interpersonal skills have been a factor in stabilizing turnover in an industry where inconsistent staffing can compromise the success of a hospitality experience.

Notwithstanding the formal management structure in place for each of the functional areas (front desk, housekeeping, maintenance and grounds, and food services), Walker is still actively involved in daily operations.

FINANCIAL PERFORMANCE

Historical financial results are recapped on attached chart detailing key financial ratios and trends. ICI enjoys the comfort of a strong balance sheet due to the substantial investment made by Walker's holding company, J.W. Holdings Inc. A debt to equity ratio of 1.02 includes postponed shareholder loans, which will remain in place.

Although operating losses have been incurred for the two years since inception ($150K and $120K respectively), ICI was able to meet its principal and interest payments before depreciation costs. Higher initial marketing costs also contributed to losses but were deemed necessary to avoid costly booking agencies and to protect revenues in future years.

ICI has been successful in achieving the target occupancy rate of 70% in its inaugural year and has generated a further 10% revenue growth in 2004. While there was some deterioration in working capital and inventory turns in 2004 (due to a $120K investment in an expanded wine cellar), wine sales are an integral aspect of revenues contributing 21% toward food and beverages income. This investment also contributed significantly to improving gross margins going into fiscal 2005.

Projections for the next year – 2005 – are based on six months interim results to date which show solid revenue and earnings performance. The projections for 2006 reflect the completion of the 15-unit cabin project after a four-month build out period and the resultant revenue/gross margin contribution.

	Mar 2003	Mar 2004	Mar 2005 forecast	Mar 2006 forecast
Revenues	$2,208	$2,429	$2,685	$3,375
GPM	48%	48%	48%	51%
Gross profit	$1,056	$1,156	$1,258	$1,709
Operating expenses	$ 700	$ 792	$ 805	$ 950
EBITDA	$ 356	$ 364	$ 453	$ 759

APPENDIX 3

COMMERCIAL LENDING

RISK ASSESSMENT

FOR

THE INN ON CORTES ISLAND LTD

COMMERCIAL LENDING RISK ASSESSMENT

OVERVIEW

A key element of the case study is Jonathan's need to obtain bank financing to complete the resort expansion. The Enterprise Review Summary (ERS), covered in Appendix 2, is a useful tactical document that will allow potential lenders to review and assess this borrowing opportunity.

Many business owners do not appreciate the depth and rigor that such applications are subjected to by commercial bank lenders.

In this Appendix, we have summarized the candid risk assessment comments from four separate commercial bankers who have reviewed the case and financial data. They all agreed that there was an opportunity to provide the additional financing but that such an expansion opportunity would have to be very carefully planned and rationalized.

We have developed a risk assessment model that consists of the following key areas:

- Financial Risk.
- Market Risk.
- Operations Risk.
- Construction Risk.
- Management Risk.

Risk concerns and issues	Mitigated by
Financial Risk	
Relatively new operation with only two years of historical cash-flow performance	Reasonable positive actual cash flow performance observed + conservative projections in place
Debt service cover (DSC) – with new debt based on historical cash-flow is inadequate	Realistic EBITDA forecasts with conservative occupancy and room rate assumptions
Tight Working Capital partly due to wine inventories and allowing drawn out A/R	A/R collection policies and Inventory management practices to be upgraded
High Total Debt: EBITDA ratio 9:1 range	Appraisal surplus mitigates to a certain extent
Increased interest rate risk during construction	Fixed interest rate guarantee can be set up
Strengthening Canadian $	Forward F/X contracts can be established
Cash flow sustainability given optimistic projected EBITDA	Sensitivity analysis, using 'worst case' scenarios, should demonstrate cash flow generation ability to cover 'interest only' on the debt
Increased Appraised value is primarily based on the forecasted future (increased) cash flows	Develop a 'second way out' via shareholder's cash flow guarantee, backed up by non- project assets?
Special use property, with no apparent alternative uses, other than a restructured resort	Cannot be mitigated aside from a strong shareholder guarantee

Risk concerns and issues	Mitigated by
Market Risk	
Remote location that is not easy to access	Well conceived marketing budget that is aimed at the right client segment who desire the remoteness attributes
Cortes Island area is not well known to travelers	Web site emphasizes the uniqueness and remoteness of the area
Tourism industry is susceptible to periodic economic downturns	Cannot mitigate fully but room rates can be discounted in worst case scenario
Established and local competitors	Local collaboration, no direct competition on the island.
Potential for Oil price shocks and negative impact on transportation costs	Upper level demographic can afford
Potential 'fickleness' of hospitality clients	Build a broad and diversified customer base, both in Canada and the USA
USA 'stay at home' concerns, post 9/11	

Risk concerns and issues	Mitigated by
Operations Risk	
Finding and retaining reliable suppliers	Ensure clients pay premium prices to preserve gross margin
Unusually high staff turnover given remote location?	Emphasize staff accommodations with frequent time off
Succession risk re Jonathan Walker	Key person insurance to be carried
Construction Risk	
Difficulty in getting reliable local construction trades	Will need to pay premium prices to trades and take this into account in the budget
Potential for construction cost overruns	Set up fixed price contracts where possible + owner has outside liquid resources to inject if need be
Management Risk	
Past discord amongst management	JW advises this has since been resolved with clearer job descriptions now in place
Difficulty in finding and keeping good management given the location	Need to pay premium salaries to retain
	Training and Development programs now in place

REFERENCES AND RECOMMENDED READINGS

Where material has been referenced and/or adapted, the necessary written permissions have been obtained from the respective publishers.

Denzil Doyle *Making Technology Happen* Silvan Communications Inc. 1997

Longenecker, Moore, Petty and Donlevy *Small Business Management – An Entrepreneurial Emphasis I.T.P.* Nelson Thomson Canada Limited 1998

Beamish and Woodcock *Strategic Management 5th ed.* McGraw Hill Ryerson Limited 1998

Industry Canada, Strategies website *Steps To Growth Capital 1999*

Lovelock, Christopher H., *Managing Services: Marketing, Operations and Human Resources, 2nd Edition.* Prentice Hall, New Jersey, 1992

Ivo Raza, *Heads in Beds: Hospitality and Tourism Marketing*

Anthony Bourdain *Kitchen Confidential, Adventures in the Culinary Underbelly* Bloomsbury Publishing, 2000

Ron Buist *Tales From Under the Rim – The Marketing of Tim Hortons* Goose Lane Editions 2003

ISBN 141207509-2

9 781412 075091